S0-BND-395

TWENTY-FIVE
ONE-ACT PLAYS

TWENTY-FIVE ONE-ACT PLAYS

by
CRANE JOHNSON

THEATRE PRESS
550 Fifth Avenue
New York 36, N. Y.

FOR

MY MOTHER *and*

FATHER

Library of Congress Catalog Card No. 66-29355

PRINTED IN UNITED STATES OF AMERICA BY
Theo. Gaus' Sons, Inc., BROOKLYN 1, N. Y.

Contents

GEORGE WASHINGTON'S CHAIR

GEORGE WASHINGTON'S CHAIR

CHARACTERS

ANNOUNCER
AMANDA PHELPS
MRS. ANDERSON
MR. HENSLEY
FIVE MEMBERS FROM THE AUDIENCE

Place: The "sitting room" of Mrs. Phelps
Time: The present

GEORGE WASHINGTON'S CHAIR

ANNOUNCER: (*Stepping out in front of curtain*) Ladies and gentlemen. There is a decision to be made in this play. An important decision for the lady who is to make it. So important, in fact, that the author decided not to let her make it alone. Instead, five members of this audience are now seated on the stage. They will watch the play themselves, consider the facts carefully, and then give the decision which will bring the play to an end. (*The Announcer steps back behind the curtains and a moment later the curtains part. We see five members of the audience seated in a row at the rear part of the stage. In front of them are two chairs and a small tea table downstage left. One of these chairs, a rocker, is being polished by Amanda Phelps. Downstage right is another straight-backed chair. Off right is a door leading to a hallway. Off left is a window. AMANDA PHELPS is in her sixties, relic of a Southern belle. Amanda is interrupted in her polishing by a bell. Her reaction is mixed. Extremely lonely, she is happy to have a visitor of any kind, but is a little unhappy that the visitor had to appear at this very busy, important time of chair polishing. Amanda rises, looks about for a place to hide her rag, finally puts it behind something on the shelf under the table, and starts off right. Before disappearing, she gives one final last look at the room and adjusts her dress a bit before disappearing off right. A moment later, Mrs. Anderson booms into the room followed by Mrs. Phelps. MRS. ANDERSON is a nondescript woman, an entity who seems incapable of having had ancestry of any kind. Mrs. Anderson is also in her sixties*)

MRS. ANDERSON: Amanda, dear, you really don't know how much I look forward to these monthly teas with you. (*Amanda flutters over and putters with something on the tea table, also checking to see that the dust rag cannot be seen*)

MRS. ANDERSON: And this dear, dear chair. (*Mrs. Anderson walks over near the chair and exclaims with her hands above it*)

MRS. ANDERSON: Why, I've never seen it in this room before.

MRS. PHELPS: There's a man coming to look at it.

MRS. ANDERSON: (*Horrified*) You mean you're thinking of selling it?

MRS. PHELPS: It's the last thing I have that's of any value.

MRS. ANDERSON: But not this . . . not this chair. Why, it'd be almost sacrilegious.

MRS. PHELPS: An antique dealer has been here twice. I wrote for him to visit me. His name is Hensley and he's made me a very good offer.

MRS. ANDERSON: Oh, but you didn't sell it! What a relief!

MRS. PHELPS: Each time he came it was because I told him to come and pick up the chair. But each time before he left, I changed my mind and made him leave without the chair.

MRS. ANDERSON: How fortunate. I mean, that you can change your mind so easily.

MRS. PHELPS: I don't know. I just don't know. (*Amanda pours tea and hands a cup to Mrs. Anderson, motioning her to sit on the important chair in question*)

MRS. ANDERSON: But not in this chair, Amanda.

MRS. PHELPS: Yes, Mrs. Anderson, in *his* chair.

MRS. ANDERSON: It'll make me too nervous, Amanda. I know I should spill the tea all over.

MRS. PHELPS: Stains won't matter, if I sell it. (*Mrs. Anderson, in almost ecstasy, sits gingerly on the rocker. Mrs. Phelps pours herself a cup of tea and sits in the chair opposite Mrs. Anderson*)

MRS. PHELPS: Rock a bit, Mrs. Anderson. It's a sturdy chair, even after all these years.

MRS. ANDERSON: I never did think I'd be rocking in this chair, knowing that even you never rock it, except once a year.

MRS. PHELPS: Yes, on *his* birthday. But this last week, I've rocked it every night before going to bed.

MRS. ANDERSON: You have! How wonderful it must have been. One can rock and think so easily of the past. Why, when I think that me, Esther Anderson, is sitting and rocking in the very same chair used by George Washington, it actually sends creeps up and down my back.

MRS. PHELPS: Yes, it helps to link one with the past. Last night I rocked for over an hour and wished I had been born back then, alive then, instead of now.

MRS. ANDERSON: I wish my cousin Min could see me now. She runs a wet wash laundry up in New Jersey.

MRS. PHELPS: (*Taking a sip of tea and beginning her dream anew. These reveries are said without regard to Mrs. Anderson*) Just about now I'd be having tea out on the wide, sprawling veranda. There would be servants to pour the tea, and more servants to take away the tea things, and more servants to adjust one's foot on the stool.

MRS. ANDERSON: Min started her business up from nothing. Used to work in a coverall laundry. Then one day she quit and started her own wash place.

MRS. PHELPS: (*Puts cup on table and rises*) I'd be wearing white silk with lots of lace and there'd be a wind in the air and the moss in the trees would dance softly with the breeze. And during tea time, there'd be a figure on horseback coming up the long veranda. Closer and closer he'd come until we'd see it was our friend George. Our best, our closest friend, George Washington.

MRS. ANDERSON: Min keeps wondering why I stay here in the South when I could come up and work with her. She promised to put me in charge of the tagging section. I'd tag the dirty clothes as they came in.

MRS. PHELPS: George would hop off his horse, kiss my hand, (*Looks down at hand*) ask about my health and inquire of my father. (*Crosses right slowly*) I'd tell him Colonel Phelps was inside, but he'd wait with me until the Colonel spotted him and called him in. Then, he'd stay over for dinner at the Phelps Mansion. The long table in the dining room would be covered with the linen the Colonel had especially made in Ireland.

MRS. ANDERSON: I remember that table cloth. The one you sold a couple years back to Nick's Spaghetti House. He cut it all up into little pieces for his greasy old tables. I was in there a couple weeks back, and I don't think he's washed those cloths since the day he cut up your linen.

MRS. PHELPS: (*At right downstage, looking far out*) The candelabras would be of shining gold and the silver would be heavy and match the plates. The table would be heaped with food of all kinds, with the servants bringing in more and more. There would be all kinds of wine glasses and the sound of people tinkling them. And after dinner there'd be dancing. Dancing in the huge drawing room under the crystal chandelier which held hundreds of flickering candles.

MRS. ANDERSON: Cousin Min's got a chandelier in her flat, but it only has seven candles and they's electric.

MRS. PHELPS: (*Still looking out right*) There'd be an orchestra playing waltzes and the happy people would dance—sometimes until the sun came up. Then, there'd be horseback riding, riding through the countryside in early morning after a dance. (*Pause*) Oh, how wonderful, how wonderful.

MRS. ANDERSON: It's a wonder a chair like this ever got rocked.

MRS. PHELPS: (*Turning to Mrs. Anderson*) That came later, when Mr. Washington was older. It was his favorite chair. Everyone knew it. Just like everyone knew Colonel Phelps was Washington's best friend.

MRS. ANDERSON: Something I've always wondered, Mrs. Phelps, how is it your married name is the same as the Colonel's?

MRS. PHELPS: Mr. Phelps was my second cousin.

MRS. ANDERSON: Oh.

MRS. PHELPS: (*Half-turn to left*) Marriage among cousins was more common in the old days than now. (*With pride*) Then, people were careful about whom they married. They were careful that their line would continue with the best possible breeding.

MRS. ANDERSON: And you're the last, ain't you?

MRS. PHELPS: (*Saying it out toward audience*) Yes, I'm

the last of the line. (*Takes step left*) And that chair is the last thing I have to remind me, to link me with the glorious past of my ancestors.

MRS. ANDERSON: I guess it makes you feel funny sometimes a-thinking back about all them people, getting born, marrying, having kids, then dying, and their kids doing the same thing, all leading down to you.

MRS. PHELPS: It gives one a feeling of pride and of responsibility.

MRS. ANDERSON: My mother came from Ireland, that's all I know about her. My old man was a carpenter who fell off a roof one day and died before I was born. But he did a lot before he died. My Ma had twelve kids, and now they're thirty-three grandchildren. All just because of a carpenter who fell off a roof one day. Makes you feel kind of funny, don't it?

MRS. PHELPS: (*Turns and starts toward chair right*) Two summers back I visited the Phelps plantation. It's called by some new name now by its owners, but old folks thereabouts still refer to it as the Phelps Mansion. I wanted to go inside, but the caretaker was very rude and sent me away.

MRS. ANDERSON: Mebbe so, but you've got this chair, and they ain't.

MRS. PHELPS: (*Sadly*) Yes, I've the chair.

MRS. ANDERSON: How could you ever think of selling it?

MRS. PHELPS: (*Sitting in chair right*) If I had money I could go away, to the city perhaps and find work. (*Pause*) There's nothing here.

MRS. ANDERSON: Move away?

MRS. PHELPS: I've no money left at all. I could never work here where people know me. I'd have to go away. The money from the chair would pay my expenses for awhile.

MRS. ANDERSON: This boarding house wouldn't seem the same without you, Mrs. Phelps. I was saying just the other day to Mrs. Rosencrantz that having you here gave class to the dump.

MRS. PHELPS: I owe board money.

MRS. ANDERSON: Oh, Mrs. Dopple understands.

MRS. PHELPS: We once had an overseer named Dopple.

MRS. ANDERSON: I guess you couldn't move and take the chair with you.

MRS. PHELPS: (*Rising and crossing behind George Washington's chair*) No. It's strange, but this little chair represents both a past and a future for me. (*Touching back of chair lovingly*) If I don't sell it to Mr. Hensley when he comes for the last time this morning, I'll still have the past with all its glories. (*Pause*) But with those glories there'll be greater and greater debts. I'm still too young to hope for an early death to solve my problems.

MRS. ANDERSON: Now, don't you talk like that!

MRS. PHELPS: And if I sell this chair, it means the past is dead forever. The link has been broken. It'll mean that I'll have money to begin a new life. A new life in a world I'll hate because of its strangeness. A new city with strangers everywhere. A job somewhere doing something I hate. (*Crosses behind chair and sits in chair down left*) Coming home at nights to a room somewhere containing nothing but cheap furniture made in some factory. Here, in this room, everything is cheap but the chair. It brings dignity, prestige, glory into this room. It radiates. And it's so comforting.

MRS. ANDERSON: (*Rocking gently*) It's got a good rocking rhythm. I'll bet Cousin Min might even buy it. She wears out two a year 'cause she's so big and fat.

MRS. PHELPS: Sometimes when I'm feeling blue and lonely, I touch his chair, oh so gently, and somehow get a new courage. It's as if my ancestors were there in that chair, along with Washington's spirit, all of them telling me to (*Pause*) keep going on. That my people were among the first in America, among the greatest.

MRS. ANDERSON: You say this Mr. Whathisname is coming this morning?

MRS. PHELPS: Yes. Oh, I don't know what to do. (*Rises and crosses slowly towards right*) I wish I could find someone to help me. Someone outside. I'm so fuddled about it, I don't know what the sensible thing to do is. (*Turning*) Oh yes, I know the sensible thing. Sell it, have money, start a new life. But there are other things. (*Right downstage, looking far out again*) Memories, sentiments. Those things are just as important. We feed not on bread alone. (*There is the sound of a bell off right. Mrs. Phelps freezes*)

MRS. ANDERSON: (*Whispering*) There he is now.

MRS. PHELPS: You answer, will you, Mrs. Anderson. And keep him in the hall for just a moment. (*Mrs. Anderson nods and exits. Mrs. Phelps goes over to the chair, touches it softly, then sinks to her knees and embraces the chair silently. She rises to her feet as she hears Mrs. Anderson and Mr. Hensley enter. Mrs. Anderson remains right stage. Mr. Hensley passes by the group of five seated in back and collects slips which have the word "yes" or "no" printed on them. He reads the slips and then puts them in his pocket*)

MR. HENSLEY: Well, Mrs. Phelps?

MRS. PHELPS: How do you do, Mr. Hensley. It was so good of you to come again.

MR. HENSLEY: My train leaves in just an hour, so this will be my last time down here.

MRS. PHELPS: You've checked those papers I told you about?

MR. HENSLEY: Yes, and it's certain without a doubt that this is the rocking chair George Washington gave your ancestor, Colonel Phelps. (*Mrs. Phelps turns and goes back behind chair, touching it as she speaks*)

MRS. PHELPS: I don't suppose, if I sold it, there'd be a way of making certain it went to a good home. I mean one where it would be . . . loved.

MR. HENSLEY: It will be auctioned off along with the rest of the things I've purchased on this trip.

MRS. PHELPS: Auctioned. Auctioned to a group of people with greedy faces and money in their hands.

MR. HENSLEY: Well, Mrs. Phelps?

MRS. PHELPS: I've dreaded this moment. Dreaded it ever since Mr. Phelps passed on. I knew it must come eventually. The moment when I'd have to choose between keeping and selling.

(*There is an alternate ending from this point on depending on group decision*)

MR. HENSLEY: After all, Mrs. Phelps, a chair's a chair and can be nothing more.

MRS. PHELPS: Yes. You are sensible, Mr. Hensley. I must be sensible also. You have the check? (*Mr. Hensley takes out a check and hands it to Mrs. Phelps who comes half-way to accept it. She folds it rather listlessly and puts it in her dress pocket. Mr. Hensley silently takes the chair and leaves. He is followed by Mrs. Anderson. Amanda waits until they've gone, then walks over and strokes the air where the chair once was. Then she wanders over and touches the cheap factory chair. As if it were fire, she recoils from it with clenched fingers. Then, she half-hurls herself into the chair, buries her face in her hands, and begins to cry softly as the curtains close*)

MR. HENSLEY: I'm really paying more than I should. I'll probably get it from the head office. The boss says I'm always paying too much just because of sentiment. He says with everything we pick up there's a tear jerker story behind it. But tears aren't cash on barrel, are they, Mrs. Phelps?

MRS. PHELPS: (*Stepping forward*) Will you have a cup of tea before you leave, Mr. Hensley?

MR. HENSLEY: There won't be time if I have to see about shipping that chair.

MRS. PHELPS: I'm not selling the chair, so there'll be time.

MR. HENSLEY: I warn you this is the last time I make the offer.

MRS. PHELPS: And the last time I'll ever offer again. Sit down, Mr. Hensley, in George Washington's chair . . . and I'll fix you a cup of tea. (*Mr. Hensley smiles and Mrs. Phelps begins fixing his tea as the curtains close*)

THE END

THE ASTONISHING MRS. O'SHAUGNESSY

THE ASTONISHING MRS. O'SHAUGNESSY

CHARACTERS

MRS. O'SHAUGNESSY
MR. O'TOOLE
FIRST THIEF
SECOND THIEF

Place: A room in an art museum
Time: A little before midnight

THE ASTONISHING MRS. O'SHAUGNESSY

(The curtain opens upon a room in a museum. It can be any room of a museum, depending on what props are available to to the director of the play. There is a doorway down left. A throne chair is upstage against the wall. The room is in semi-darkness, with a little light coming down from an overhead window which is not visible to the audience. After a moment, two shadowy characters enter from off right. They are two thieves. The FIRST THIEF is a slim, middle-aged thief with a haughty bearing about him. The SECOND THIEF is short, fat, and highly ignorant. They have never been of any use to themselves or to anyone else, and are two characters who would not be missed from any level of society. In the interest of the play, they are never to be played sympathetically. The First Thief motions for the Second Thief to follow him.)

SECOND THIEF: Is dis the room, Joe?

FIRST THIEF: Shh! The way you talk you'd think you wuz a lecture guide here in the museum instead of a common burglar.

SECOND THIEF: (*Highly offended*) Ah, you shouldn't have said that, Joe. *Common.* Dat hurts. Da only reason I tagged onto you is 'cause you convinced me you were different. Not afraid to bump off anyone which gets in your way. And high class. You know, 'cause you're always knocking off museums, and art galleries, and other ritzy joints. Like tonight, for instance, with us here after them Egyptian jewels.

FIRST THIEF: Why I ever choosed you for a partner for this museum job I'll never know. Gee, I should have my head zipped open and examined for picking such a dumb lout.

SECOND THIEF: I'll be quieter after this, Joe. Honest. Like a mouse in a barn what knows there's a cat around. That's how quiet I'll be.

FIRST THIEF: O. K. You can start right now. (*The First Thief steps to his left and looks around*)

SECOND THIEF: (*Barely audible*) Is dis the jewels room?

FIRST THIEF: What? I can't hear you.

SECOND THIEF: Gee, Joe, I speak so's you can hear me and you say I'm screaming, and when I whispers like you want me to, you can't hear me at all!

FIRST THIEF: Don't say nothin'. If anything brilliant goes through that scrawny eggshell head of yours, write it down and hand it to me later. Or better yet, mail it to me, pigeon-express! (*The First Thief takes out a small pocket flashlight and flashes it around the room*)

SECOND THIEF: (*Stepping forward*) Ain't that light risky, Joe? I ain't criticisn', just askin'.

FIRST THIEF: The way I got it doped out, that old watchman is down fixing coffee for hisself. (*Checks watch*) He's fixed it just about this time for the last eight nights.

SECOND THIEF: And what about the scrubwoman?

FIRST THIEF: Her name's O'Shaugnessy. Mrs. O'Shaugnessy. Tonight's her night off.

SECOND THIEF: Are you sure?

FIRST THIEF: Sure I'm sure. And even if it weren't, the old lady's harmless. Nutty as a hootowl. Spent two years once in a booby hatch.

SECOND THIEF: How come she's working here?

FIRST THIEF: 'Cause she never hurts nobody, that's why!

SECOND THIEF: I'm sorry I asked.

FIRST THIEF: So am I. Now, let's stop the gabbing, and git to work. All them Egyptian jewels is somewhere in this museum wing, in one of these rooms. (*The First Thief flashes his light around, but quickly turns it off when he hears a noise off right*)

FIRST THIEF: There's someone coming. Quick, into the next room! (*Both thieves are silent for a moment, then dash through door into room off left. A moment later, Mr. O'Toole enters. O'TOOLE is the nightwatchman, a man in his middle sixties. He is whistling rather softly—an Irish air. After looking around the room, with the aid of his flashlight, he enters through the door off left. There is a sound of a crash, followed by a groan, then silence. After a moment the two thieves reenter, but disappear back into the room as they see something from the right approaching them. It is Mrs. O'Shaugnessy. The lights on the stage come up as the moon shines overhead. The sound of music can now be heard. It is the beginning part of Entry of the Gladiators. MRS. O'SHAUGNESSY is by nature a dumpy woman in her early sixties, looking Irish, and with an Irish brogue. However, now, she is dressed as an Egyptian queen carrying, however, a wash bucket with some hand brushes exposed in her right hand. Her face is painted in the Egyptian manner and her walk may not be queenly but it is a good facsimile. An extra word or two about this lady might aid in her characterization. Mrs. O'Shaugnessy is a nobody who does not particularly care for this world where nobodies are nobodies. So, she finds her pleasure in escape. Six nights a week she is the most diligent scrubber of floors at the Art Museum. Her one night a week off is usually spent at the Museum where she escapes into a harmless sort of madness whereby she recreates a figure in some particular period of history. Mrs. O'Shaugnessy's knowledge of the past and its events is far from accurate in any sense. Most of her knowledge has been picked up from scraps of comment, cards in showcases, etc. To this scanty knowledge, she has mixed a vivid imagination. Tonight, Mrs. O'Shaugnessy has stripped some Egyptian gear off a dummy and is a queen from ten until twelve. The authorities of the museum pretend not to notice Mrs. O'Shaugnessy's off-night escapades because her loyalty has been long unquestioned. The lady saves all she can from her scrub salary so she can be listed amongst the highest cash contributing patrons of the museum. Mrs. O'Shaugnessy is also leaving what money she has to the institution, so it is with a great kindness that she is tolerated. Now, back to the action! The burglars have reentered momentarily, only to duck back into the room off left upon hearing (or viewing) Mrs. O'Shaugnessy. After posing dramatically at her entrance, Mrs. O'Shaugnessy marches majestically around the room to the music, which soon fades. It is important that, although Mrs. O'Shaugnessy seems ludicrous to us, she carry herself with the utmost possible dignity)*

MRS. O'SHAUGNESSY: Yoo Hoo. Oh, Prince O'Toole. Oh, Crown Prince O'Toole. (*Mrs. O'Shaugnessy is obviously disappointed at not seeing Mr. O'Toole, who, unbeknown to her, is out cold in the next room*)

MRS. O'SHAUGNESSY: Are you hiding, Prince O'Toole from Nefret-ity, the great Egyptian Queen of the Nile? Are you in the wind-blown, yellow rushes by the rippling green waters? Beware of the green-backed, red-eyed alligators lurking there. They are not to be trusted. I once had a pet alligator who followed my little boat as I cruised romantically Sunday afternoons on the Nile. Sometimes I used to pet him with my lovely, little hand, and he would purr so contentedly. But one Sunday afternoon, as I was petting him, he bit off my hand. How I scolded him! Fortunately, it grew back and the next time I saw him there was a great sorrowful look in his eyes. He wept tears of gratitude. I knew he was sorry for what he had done and I forgave him. Pompavius was his name and he lived to be several hundred years old which indeed was miraculous, considering how I had to nurse him so carefully just after he was born. (*Mrs. O'Shaugnessy moves about the room*) Come, Crown Prince O'Toole, come, I have two clear-eyed, trusty dromedary camels waiting for our trip to the pyramids. The tall, tall pyramids which wait patiently in the desert sands near the little oases where palm trees sway in the evening breeze. Come, come, let us inspect our tombs where, when we are dead, we shall lie as dusty, dusty mummies until the American museum people come to dig us up. Oh, Mr. O'Toole . . . (*The two thieves enter the room cautiously, not knowing quite what they'll do to Mrs. O'Shaugnessy. When Mrs. O'Shaugnessy sees them, she seems delighted*)

MRS. O'SHAUGNESSY: Oh, how do you do? Have you seen the Crown Prince? I left him just a moment ago by the marshes of the cool, ripple-rippling Nile, and now he's disappeared.

FIRST THIEF: (*Cautiously*) You must be the scrubwoman, Mrs. O'Shaugnessy.

MRS. O'SHAUGNESSY: I am Nefret-ity, Egyptian Queen

of the Nile, eighteenth dynasty, 1375 years B.C., who has a thousand captured slaves of all colors, and a green-backed pet alligator who is named Pompavius.

SECOND THIEF: She talks like a cuckoo clock!

FIRST THIEF: Shh!

SECOND THIEF: Let's take care of her, the same way we did that nightwatchman.

FIRST THIEF: No.

SECOND THIEF: Just a wee, itsy-bitsy sort of tap?

FIRST THIEF: What good would she be to us out cold?

SECOND THIEF: Ya ain't gonna let her traipse around in that crazy costume, spying on us!

FIRST THIEF: She may know where the Egyptian jewels are hidden. I plan to use psychology. She's so dumb it'll be like playing with putty in my hands. When you're lucky enough to be born with brains, you're supposed to use them, and that's what *I'm* gonna do.

SECOND THIEF: Psy, psy, Psychology?

FIRST THIEF: Yeah. And if that don't work we'll give her the same treatment we gave that old watchman in the next room.

SECOND THIEF: Ah, let's don't take no chances, Joe. I vote we give it to her now. 'Sides, I gits a kick hittin' people on their heads. Makes the funniest sound, like plunkin' a cantaloupe to see if it's ripe. Ever notice?

FIRST THIEF: I hate cantaloupes.

SECOND THIEF: Oh, Gee, I'm sorry. I like cantaloupes myself, but others . . .

FIRST THIEF: Can the yap! (*To Mrs. O'Shaugnessy*) So, you're the Egyptian Queen of the Nile?

MRS. O'SHAUGNESSY: You haven't kidnapped the Crown Prince and hidden him in the giant ear of the silent Sphinx?

FIRST THIEF: Naw, why would we want to do that?

MRS. O'SHAUGNESSY: Because he wears the rare diamond and ruby jewel of Osiris. (*The Second Thief turns to go back to Mr. O'Toole to inspect him, but the First Thief pulls him back*)

FIRST THIEF: It's all in her head, you dope. That night watchman ain't wearin' nothin' of value.

MRS. O'SHAUGNESSY: Yes, you've kidnapped him. I'm sure of it. If you don't bring him back, I'll send word to my alligator friend in the Nile and he and all his sharp-jawed friends will chase you out of Egypt, across the sandy white desert to the shores of the wind-blown blue Mediterranean where the shiny black whales wait to gobble you up with their pearly white teeth.

SECOND THIEF: Let me konk her now. Please, purty please?

FIRST THIEF: Shh! (*To Mrs. O'Shaugnessy*) Ya got us wrong, Queenie. We ain't after the Crown Prince. We're your friends.

MRS. O'SHAUGNESSY: You're strange. Not from Egypt. Foreigners. From where?

FIRST THIEF: A strange land.

MRS. O'SHAUGNESSY: Where?

FIRST THIEF: America.

MRS. O'SHAUGNESSY: I've never heard of this land.

FIRST THIEF: That's probably 'cause it ain't been discovered yet.

MRS. O'SHAUGNESSY: Oh. Yes, that's very logical. Well, do you come as ambassadors?

FIRST THIEF: Yes. We have arrived to save Egypt from a terrible hoax.

MRS. O'SHAUGNESSY: Hoax?

FIRST THIEF: Yes, for we have discovered all your crown jewels are fake.

MRS. O'SHAUGNESSY: (*In agony*) Oh, no!

FIRST THIEF: But the previous owners of these fakes will match them with real jewels if I bring them back.

MRS. O'SHAUGNESSY: Oh, this is indeed a blow to me. Please, won't you bring that throne over to me so I may rest a bit. The shock, you know! (*The Second Thief brings throne and Mrs. O'Shaugnessy seats herself majestically*) Dear me, many times have I petted Pompavius, my pet alligator, on the head with my little white fingers decked with flashing gold and sparkling rubies, not knowing they weren't real. Perhaps that is why he bit my hand off.

FIRST THIEF: It sounds very probable.

SECOND THIEF: How could a hand grow back?

FIRST THIEF: Shh. (*To Mrs. O'Shaugnessy*) The Crown Prince must not know of this. It would only worry him.

MRS. O'SHAUGNESSY: Oh, indeed it would worry him. He has ulcers already.

FIRST THIEF: Not really!

MRS. O'SHAUGNESSY: And he's still quite young, don't you think?

FIRST THIEF: Young, yes, but not so young as you, I think.

MRS. O'SHAUGNESSY: Flatterer! My, I wish Pompavius were here. He'd be jealous! And his red eyes flash so, when he's jealous!

FIRST THIEF: Of course the jewels are carefully hidden?

MRS. O'SHAUGNESSY: Oh, yes.

FIRST THIEF: Here in . . .

MRS. O'SHAUGNESSY: Yes, here in this great temple. The ancient temple of Osiris, our god, you know, whom we worship with much glorious pageantry and red, bloody, gory sacrifice.

SECOND THIEF: Hey, let me shut her off. One little tap. It's getting late!

FIRST THIEF: Your royal majesty.

MRS. O'SHAUGNESSY: Yes?

FIRST THIEF: There's a north wind blowing from the Nile.

MRS. O'SHAUGNESSY: Yes, isn't there. How nice. Shall we stroll along the honey-dew banks where the weeping weeping willow trees caress the gentle laughing waters.

FIRST THIEF: My little wooden sailboat awaits me and I need a north wind.

MRS. O'SHAUGNESSY: What color sail?

FIRST THIEF: What color?

MRS. O'SHAUGNESSY: Yes, what color?

SECOND THIEF: Pink. (*The Second Thief looks a little foolish as he realizes he's supplied the answer*)

MRS. O'SHAUGNESSY: Pink! Oh, I love pink. Pink sails puffed out in the breeze. Sailing, sailing, with no noise save the pure ivory oars dipping in, dipping out, in and out of the blue, blue, deep-blue ocean. How lovely!

FIRST THIEF: Soon the wind will be from the south.

MRS. O'SHAUGNESSY: Oh, that awful south wind. Brings all the smells from the brewery. I see now why you are anxious.

FIRST THIEF: The jewels are carefully hidden?

MRS. O'SHAUGNESSY: Oh, yes. No one knows where they are.

FIRST THIEF: (*Dejected*) Oh.

MRS. O'SHAUGNESSY: Except me.

FIRST THIEF: You do!

MRS. O'SHAUGNESSY: It's a secret no one knows. I mean, about me knowing where they're hidden. I was here one night when the high priest brought them out to show to some friends. Then, he put them back.

FIRST THIEF: (*Becoming excited*) Put them back?

MRS. O'SHAUGNESSY: Yes, in the oddest place. (*Titters*) You'd never guess in a million years.

SECOND THIEF: We could torture her, huh?

FIRST THIEF: (*To Mrs. O'Shaugnessy*) Let's not waste time guessing. You'll show me the jewels?

MRS. O'SHAUGNESSY: Yes. But, first, you have to deliver back to me Crown Prince O'Toole. I feel sure you've kidnapped him.

FIRST THIEF: Honest we ain't.

SECOND THIEF: Cross our hearts and hope to die!

MRS. O'SHAUGNESSY: I wish Pompavius were here. He would know what to do.

FIRST THIEF: I have a very good idea where the Crown Prince is.

MRS. O'SHAUGNESSY: You do!

FIRST THIEF: He's with Pompavius.

MRS. O'SHAUGNESSY: With Pompavius! Oh, how happy

those words are to me. You know, they've been on unfriendly terms for the longest period. The Crown Prince is a very nice person but not the most understanding. One day, in a playful mood, Pompavius swallowed the leg of the Crown Prince. I made him give it back right away, but the Crown Prince was greatly vexed. But now they are friends again. Where are they?

FIRST THIEF: In a secret hiding place.

SECOND THIEF: We'll tell you where when we've got the jewels.

MRS. O'SHAUGNESSY: Oh, how nice. I love games!

FIRST THIEF: You'll tell us where the jewels are?

MRS. O'SHAUGNESSY: Yes, they're in the very next room. (*Mrs. O'Shaugnessy points to her right. The Second Thief begins to run in that direction, but is stopped by his comrade*)

FIRST THIEF: Your majesty, where in the next room?

MRS. O'SHAUGNESSY: In a secret drawer hidden in two Egyptian mummy coffins.

SECOND THIEF: Mummy coffins!

MRS. O'SHAUGNESSY: Yes, if you'll bring them in here, I'll show you where.

SECOND THIEF: But coffins! (*To First Thief*) Say, let's slug this dame and really look!

MRS. O'SHAUGNESSY: The cases are very light, even though their walls are very thick. (*Both men look at one another, shrug, and then exit off right. Mrs. O'Shaugnessy, when alone, begins talking to herself*)

MRS. O'SHAUGNESSY: (*Rising*) How annoying it is to know one has been tricked. The jewels looked so real. Really nowadays one cannot tell the real from the unreal. I'm *sure* now that was why Pompavius was upset that day he ate my arm. It was meant as a sign to me that the jewels were false. My, how surprised the Crown Prince will be when he finds I've secured the genuine jewels in place of the false. Then, there will be great celebrating. My thousand slaves will form a blazing torchlight processional carrying me on a golden throne high, high above the others. The fiery flames from their torches will shoot high, high upwards into the black, black sky. And the chains around the slaves' ankles will be clanking and the people everywhere will be cheering. Cheering for me. For me, they'll be cheering. Down through the streets we'll go. Down to the river Nile, the ancient river Nile, where my boat will be awaiting, streamers flying proudly from all the masts. And there'll be fireworks of all colors. Crimson red, jade green, and bursting yellow. All will flash brightly in the air above me, and Pompavious and all his little friends will be following me. And, if I'm in a merry mood, I shall, perhaps, have slaves jump into the water so that the hungry alligators will enjoy the festivities as much as I. My, my, how wonderful it is to be Nefret-ity, the great queen of Egypt. (*The two thieves return carrying two large mummy cases*)

SECOND THIEF: These the ones, your majesty?

MRS. O'SHAUGNESSY: The very ones. Please place them on the floor, side by side. That's right. Now open them.

SECOND THIEF: Open them! Gee, maybe someone's inside. I mean . . .

FIRST THIEF: (*Sarcastically*) Why don't you knock and see? (*The Second Thief, in a serious manner, knocks, much to the contempt of the First Thief*)

MRS. O'SHAUGNESSY: It's no use knocking. The wood is so thick they would not hear you, or you hear them. Besides, the coffins are empty. They are to be used for the Crown Prince and myself when we are dead and turned into mummies. Aren't they lovely coffins? Do you think the American museum keepers will like them?

FIRST THIEF: Sure, sure! But about the drawers?

MRS. O'SHAUGNESSY: Open both lids. (*Both thieves open the lids, the Second Thief a little nervously. When the lids are open, the Second Thief looks over to peer inside. Just as he does so, the First Thief says "Boo" which startles his comrade*)

SECOND THIEF: Ah, Joe, whydja have to do that for? You know I'm the noivous type.

FIRST THIEF: Your royal highness, there ain't nothin' inside. I mean jewels or nothin'.

MRS. O'SHAUGNESSY: Of course not. (*Titters*) The drawers are located in a false bottom and are opened and closed by a carefully balanced weight system.

SECOND THIEF: Whadya know!

MRS. O'SHAUGNESSY: Invented by Mr. Einstein, the genius.

SECOND THIEF: (*To First Thief*) Was he Egyptian?

FIRST THIEF: Shh! How do these weights operate?

MRS. O'SHAUGNESSY: Very simply. Each of you two gentlemen place a hand in the center of each coffin bottom and push when I say three. (*Both men do as directed and wait for the counting*)

MRS. O'SHAUGNESSY: One, two, three, push! (*Both men push, but nothing happens. Mrs. O'Shaugnessy is a little distressed*)

MRS. O'SHAUGNESSY: That's strange.

FIRST THIEF: You're sure there're drawers in these coffins?

MRS. O'SHAUGNESSY: Positive. Perhaps more weight is needed. Suppose each of you puts one of his feet in. And I'll count again. (*The two thieves put in their feet and Mrs. O'Shaugnessy begins the counting again*)

MRS. O'SHAUGNESSY: One, two, three, push! (*Again, nothing happens*)

SECOND THIEF: Ah, Joe, the woman's a looney. You told me yourself. Look what we're doin'. She'll have us being looneys along with her. Let me give her just one itsy-bitsy sort of a konk on the head, so we can really look. Please?

MRS. O'SHAUGNESSY: The men who opened it last time were much heavier and they balanced their weight equally over the false bottom.

FIRST THIEF: You mean, it has to be balanced over the whole area?

MRS. O'SHAUGNESSY: Yes. (*Titters*) I guess I forgot to tell you.

FIRST THIEF: (*Brightening*) That sounds logical. Get in the coffin, Edgar.

SECOND THIEF: Oh, no! (*After a dirty look from Joe, Edgar crawls into the coffin*)

FIRST THIEF: Now, lie down on your belly and see what happens.

SECOND THIEF: Oh, Joe, I seen too many of them horror pictures. I'm scared. 'Sides, you knows I'm full of superstitions! (*A look from Joe prompts Edgar to fall on his belly. Nothing happens*)

FIRST THIEF: Try bouncing up and down. (*Edgar bounces up and down, but nothing happens*)

FIRST THIEF: Look, Mrs. O'Shaugnessy. I mean, your highness. He's in the mummy coffin like you say, but still nothing happens.

MRS. O'SHAUGNESSY: (*Tittering*) That's because the coffin's only one half of a pair.

FIRST THIEF: Whadya mean?

MRS. O'SHAUGNESSY: The balancin' has got to be equal in both coffins.

FIRST THIEF: How come? They ain't connected.

MRS. O'SHAUGNESSY: (*Seriously*) I think it's something to do with radar.

FIRST THIEF: Oh.

SECOND THIEF: Say Joe, can I climb out now?

FIRST THIEF: Back on your belly, and shut up. (*The First Thief climbs into the remaining coffin, talking to Mrs. O'Shaugnessy as he does so*)

FIRST THIEF: Look, your majesty, when I'm flat, you start counting again. And Edgar, hey, Edgar, you listenin'?

SECOND THIEF: (*Face peering out of coffin*) I'm too scared to listen.

FIRST THIEF: When her highness counts to three, start bouncing on your belly. Understand?

SECOND THIEF: Ah, Joe, this is so silly!

FIRST THIEF: On your belly! (*Both thieves are on their stomachs and Mrs. O'Shaugnessy begins counting again*)

MRS. O'SHAUGNESSY: One, two, three, push! (*Some movement is observed coming from the coffin, but no drawers open. The First Thief looks out of the coffin*)

FIRST THIEF: Anything happen?

MRS. O'SHAUGNESSY: Dear me, no.

FIRST THIEF: Look Queenie, you couldn't be spoofin' us?

MRS. O'SHAUGNESSY: Why, no, I remember it so clearly from the last time.

SECOND THIEF: I'm gettin' an awfully strange feeling inside of me. Like somethin' terrible's about to happen. Let's come back some other night, huh?

FIRST THIEF: Look, your majesty, are we doing anything different? Try and remember.

MRS. O'SHAUGNESSY: I'm trying.

FIRST THIEF: Can you remember things them guys—the priests and his entourage—about what they said.

MRS. O'SHAUGNESSY: Not exactly, except that they kept saying it must be perfectly balanced—that the least little thing throws it off.

SECOND THIEF: Maybe this gun of mine throws it off balance. Here, Queenie, you hold it. (*The Second Thief hands his revolver to Mrs. O'Shaugnessy*)

FIRST THIEF: Yeah, maybe that's it. (*The First Thief hands his revolver to Mrs. O'Shaugnessy*)

FIRST THIEF: Naw, that ain't it. We were balanced 'cause there was two revolvers. (*Mrs. O'Shaugnessy, not knowing what to do with the revolvers, places them under the cushion of the throne. Both men seem lost in their thoughts. The First Thief suddenly snaps his fingers*)

FIRST THIEF: I've got it!

SECOND THIEF: (*Head out of coffin*) The jewelry?

FIRST THIEF: No, stupid. I know what's wrong. Tell me, your highness, this last time you were here, were the lids up or down. I mean, open or closed?

MRS. O'SHAUGNESSY: Why, open, I believe.

FIRST THIEF: Are you certain?

MRS. O'SHAUGNESSY: If they were closed one wouldn't be able to breathe.

SECOND THIEF: You could in mine. Maybe you couldn't be heard, but there're enough cracks letting in the air.

FIRST THIEF: Same thing with my coffin. Enough air coming in for breathing.

MRS. O'SHAUGNESSY: I do wish I could remember.

FIRST THIEF: It's worth experimenting with the lids down. We'll have to practice counting together, Edgar, so's we'll bounce at the same time.

SECOND THIEF: If this don't work, can I do the old lady in? On account of wasting our time like this?

FIRST THIEF: Sure. (*Rising*) As soon as we get the jewels, you can bash the old hag's skull in. Then, do the same with that nightwatchman out there. They're just old people. Dumb and stupid. Worthless. While we, we're smart, plenty smart. Why, when we get these jewels, we'll be riding high. I got big plans for us ahead. But, the jewels come first now. After we get them, you can kill these two old people any way your little heart desires.

SECOND THIEF: Gee, tanks.

FIRST THIEF: (*Kneeling*) Now, begin counting! (*The First Thief nods and then both thieves practice counting until they have established an agreed-upon rhythm*)

FIRST THIEF: Well, we're ready, your majesty. Wish us luck.

MRS. O'SHAUGNESSY: Oh, I wish the Crown Prince and Pompavius were here. How they would love the suspense.

FIRST THIEF: Let's start the counting, Edgar, and start hitting every time we say three. It may take some time, so have patience. Into our coffins! One, two, three! (*Both men begin counting, drop into coffins, and pull lids over them. Mrs. O'Shaugnessy stands for a moment and then sees a small drawer coming out of the coffin nearest her. She reaches down, takes something out of the drawer, puts it in her bodice, and closes the drawer back into the coffin. At this moment, Mr. O'Toole enters from off left rubbing his head. Mrs. O'Shaugnessy turns as she hears him*)

MRS. O'SHAUGNESSY: Oh, there you are, Crown Prince O'Toole. You ran away from me, you naughty boy!

MR. O'TOOLE: You know that old lead vase up on the shelf in the next room?

MRS. O'SHAUGNESSY: Indeed I do. It's from my own tomb

in the pyramid. The Germans dug it up and the Americans bought it.

MR. O'TOOLE: I always had a hunch it'd fall on somebody, and tonight it fell on me. Guess I slammed the door too hard. Must have knocked me out for a whole minute or so. But I'm all right now. Well, that's quite a get-up you've got on, Mrs. O'Shaugnessy.

MRS. O'SHAUGNESSY: If you please, I am Nefret-ity, the Empress Queen of Egypt. Ruler of the Nile and all her possessions.

MR. O'TOOLE: I liked you better last week as Marie Antoinette. Well, the coffee should be percolating by now. Will you come down and join me, your majesty?

MRS. O'SHAUGNESSY: I shall be honored, Crown Prince.

MR. O'TOOLE: Nothin' happened while I was out . . . out, that's a good one! I mean, nothin' stirrin'?

MRS. O'SHAUGNESSY: Let me see . . .

MR. O'TOOLE: What're these Egyptian mummy cases doing here on the floor? Bertha, did you . . . (*Mrs. O'Shaugnessy hangs her head*)

MR. O'TOOLE: Oh, that's all right. They're to be cleaned inside tomorrow anyway, so we'll just leave them here where they are. Of course, the clasps should be down. (*Mr. O'Toole walks over and drops the clasp on each coffin lid*)

MRS. O'SHAUGNESSY: They were part of a story I was imagin'. Sometimes the things I imagine seem as real as life. About the coffins, I don't know how they got in here.

MR. O'TOOLE: Forget it, Bertha. So, tonight, you're Queen of the Nile.

MRS. O'SHAUGNESSY: And you're the Crown Prince.

MR. O'TOOLE: And I'm the Crown Prince. Your son or your brother?

MRS. O'SHAUGNESSY: Whichever you like.

MR. O'TOOLE: I'll think about it on the way down. Coming, your majesty?

MRS. O'SHAUGNESSY: Oh, yes, Crown Prince, and I have a surprise for tonight.

MR. O'TOOLE: A surprise will help things, being as how it's sort of boring working around a museum, with nothing ever happening. What's the surprise, your royal highness? (*Mrs. O'Shaugnessy reaches into her bodice and takes out the package she took from the Egyptian coffin*)

MRS. O'SHAUGNESSY: Sardines. I've been saving them for a special occasion. Tonight ain't, but we can pretend, can't we?

MR. O'TOOLE: Sure, your majesty. We can pretend. (*The music of Entry of the Gladiators begins again. Mr. O'Toole picks up Mrs. O'Shaugnessy's train, and she circles the stage and exits right as the curtains close*)

THE END

THE PROPOSAL

THE PROPOSAL

CHARACTERS

MRS. GLADYS POMPEROY: A widow in her early sixties
HUBERT POMPEROY: Her son
MRS. EDNA HIGBY: Her daughter
LYSANDER GREEN: Her lover
CLOETTE: Her French maid

Place: The bedroom of Mrs. Pomperoy
Time: The present

THE PROPOSAL

(The scene is the very luxurious bedroom of Mrs. Gladys Pomperoy. Downstage center is a satin lounge. To the right is a door leading to other parts of the house. Upstage right, against the wall, is a bureau of drawers. Upstage back, against the wall, is a writing desk. A window is in the wall left. Just before the curtains part, we hear the loud wailing of Gladys, and when the curtains do part we see her sitting on the satin lounge, crying profusely. GLADYS is in her early sixties, carefully preserved with much paint. Standing to the right of the lounge is Edna, while Hubert stands to the left of the lounge. HUBERT is an extremely dull person in his middle thirties, completely lacking in imagination of any kind. EDNA is his female counterpart, a year or so older.)

GLADYS: You see what you've done! This is the precious little silk embroidered handkerchief dear Mrs. Arnold sent me all the way from Naples, and the colors are beginning to run.

HUBERT: (*Short of patience*) Well, if you'd stop that . . . blubbering.

GLADYS: Blubbering! (*This starts Gladys crying anew. Edna gives Hubert an angry look, crosses to the bureau right and takes out a fresh handkerchief, crosses back, and hands it to her mother*)

GLADYS: (*To Edna*) Thank you, dear. I can't understand it. Most of the time you're so sweet to your mother, but in times like this, I just don't know . . .

HUBERT: It's for your own good, Mother. Edna and I have no intention of hurting you. It's just that you're growing older and we're trying to protect you, that's all.

GLADYS: But I don't want to be protected!

EDNA: We know you don't, Mother. That's why we've been so careful about . . . looking after you. You must realize you're getting on in years and that your . . . judgment . . . may not be as keen as it once was.

GLADYS: Judgment! No one ever questioned my judgment when I married your father. The dullest man in town, but I knew he had a capacity, a capacity which has made us a very wealthy family. If it weren't for my . . . judgment, you'd both be out working instead of living off my . . . early judgments.

HUBERT: Now, mother . . .

GLADYS: I'm tired of having my life run for me by others. Tired of this house where *you* choose my friends and stand about me as if you were keepers. I've stood it just about as long as I'm going to.

EDNA: Mother, we know the kind of people our money attracts. All kinds, and some not very pleasant.

GLADYS: I know you're referring to . . . Lysander. Please don't categorize him.

EDNA: I can't understand how that man has entrapped you.

GLADYS: He has not entrapped . . .

HUBERT: (*Showing papers*) Here are his records. In cold, black and white print. *Must* we read them again!

GLADYS: Lysander Green is the sincerest, kindest, most understanding, most misunderstood man I've ever known. He has so many of those dear, dear qualities your father lacked.

HUBERT: Like murdering his wives, for instance?

GLADYS: There's no proof.

EDNA: He's had four wives, Mother, all of whom died mysteriously. One so mysteriously that he spent two years in prison for it.

GLADYS: How horrible those two years must have been.

EDNA: Why don't you try seeing it from the wives' point of view.

GLADYS: If it *is* true, then there must have been good reasons. Lysander is *so* reasonable.

HUBERT: The reasons are simple. Pure and simple. Money. This Lysander Green of yours has made his profession marrying rich widows and then murdering them.

GLADYS: I still say, there is no proof!

EDNA: All right, Mother. Perhaps he didn't murder them. But they all died just a year after they'd married this Mr.

Green. Doesn't that strike you as being more than . . . coincidental?

GLADYS: If you only knew him as *I* do. Edna, dear, go to the desk and bring me that little pink box with the blue ribbons on it. (*Edna obliges and hands her mother the box. Gladys sighs and then begins taking out some letters*)

GLADYS: Yes, if you only knew him as I do. Such beautiful letters. I just won't believe it's possible for a man who's so poetic to be cruel in any way. (*Looking through one letter*) Why, in just this line, he says I'm "like a luscious fruit upon a bow, grown ripe, and ready to be plucked." (*Gladys sighs*)

HUBERT: (*Disgustedly*) Ready to be plucked! I guess that's true all right. He's surely out to pluck you.

GLADYS: You don't follow the metaphor. He's comparing youth as . . . green apples on a tree, while I, who am older, am red and ripe, ready to be bitten into. (*Flustered*) Well, I guess I *am* carrying the metaphor too far. But, you see what I mean.

HUBERT: Mother, Edna and I have decided that this affair must come to an end. Quickly and completely. You are not to see this Lysander Green any more.

GLADYS: But he's brought me such happiness. Such happiness. And, my dears, he's so charming. *Even* Mrs. Vandergripp thinks he's charming, and you know how hard *she* is to please. And his voice, so romantic. (*Sighing*) Whenever he speaks, I see pictures of Venetian gondolas in the moonlight. I hear soft violins. And, somewhere, far away, come the fragile rhapsodies of a celestial choir. (*Sighing*) And his gentleness. The way he bows and takes my hand, touching and caressing it as if it were the most precious little hand in the world. Oh, my children, you can't understand. Lysander's made life worth living again.

EDNA: Well, you've got to forget all about him, Mother. We'll talk no more about it. And if you're going to be . . . difficult, Hubert and I will have to take . . . measures of some kind. (*Edna turns to go. Before Edna reaches the door, however, CLOETTE, the maid, enters*)

CLOETTE: Mrs. Pomperoy, your Mr. Green is here. (*Gladys lights up*)

EDNA: Tell him my mother is not at home and he's not to bother her any more.

GLADYS: (*Pleading*) Edna!

HUBERT: Do as my sister says, Cloette, and be quick about it.

CLOETTE: The gentleman followed me in, sir, and I suspect he's just outside the hall hearing all this.

GLADYS: Oh, my dear Lysander. His feelings are probably being bruised. (*To Edna and Hubert*) Let me talk to him, please.

EDNA: Mother, you're not to see him again, ever.

GLADYS: I know I shall have a nervous breakdown if I don't see him this time.

HUBERT: Well . . .

EDNA: We'll let you see him, Mother, if you promise that after he's gone out through that door, you'll have no more to do with him.

GLADYS: Is that the *only* way I may see him?

HUBERT: The only way.

GLADYS: (*Sighing*) Then, let it be.

EDNA: Hubert and I shall be in the next room to see that he goes out alone and for good. Cloette, you may show this . . . show him in. (*Cloette curtsies and leaves. In a moment Cloette reenters with Lysander Green. Both Edna and Hubert give Lysander fiery stares and then exit. LYSANDER is in his early sixties, a tall, silver-haired romantic figure, dashingly dressed. When he sees he is alone with Gladys, he rushes over, kneels, and kisses her hand. Gladys is ecstatic, but then remembers her mission*)

GLADYS: Did you kiss the . . . *others* this way, Lysander.

LYSANDER: Others?

GLADYS: Your first four wives. I know, dear. My children have had you investigated.

LYSANDER: (*Rising*) Four? Were there only four?

GLADYS: You don't remember?

LYSANDER: I remember love, only love. (*Turning right*) One forgets the love objects and remembers only the love.

GLADYS: My daughter, Edna, says they all died mysteriously.

LYSANDER: Why, not at all. (*Walking left behind the lounge seat*) Hazel slipped in the bathtub one night and drowned. (*Thinking*) Geraldine fell from our second story window one morning, down into the patio where all my prize geraniums were kept. (*Thoughtfully*) Broke three pots. (*Stepping left*) Margaret tripped and fell off an ocean liner during a heavy fog as we were coming into Le Havre. (*Stepping left*) And poor Gwendolyn, she locked herself in the closet one night by mistake and we didn't hear her cries until after she'd been dead for three days.

GLADYS: Poor Gwendolyn.

LYSANDER: (*Turning right*) But *none* died *mysteriously,* as you see. It's a shame your children wasted that money investigating.

GLADYS: The report said you were in prison.

LYSANDER: Two years. Ghastly!

GLADYS: For what cause, dear?

LYSANDER: It was something to do with Hazel's death, or was it with Geraldine's? I can't recall. Anyway, they gave me two years . . . for negligence.

GLADYS: How it grieves me, dear Lysander, to think of you there . . . in prison.

LYSANDER: Please don't, Gladys. There was a lady matron who made life . . . bearable. Unfortunately, she died just a week before my release. Helen was her name.

GLADYS: And now you've selected me.

LYSANDER: Yes, you. (*Lysander sits next to Gladys*)

GLADYS: I suspect though, Lysander, that you're interested . . . in my money.

LYSANDER: Why, of course, Gladys. It is the most . . . charming thing about you. I can only continue being in love with love as long as my love objects have the means.

GLADYS: Oh, Lysander, how honest you are. So honest and noble. (*Turning out*) I can't understand why my children dislike you so.

LYSANDER: Some people have a strange sense of values.

GLADYS: Yes, that's true. Tell me, Lysander, were your wives happy?

LYSANDER: Oh, sublimely so. I made each of their years a divine experience. Gwendolyn had led such a dull life until she met me.

GLADYS: I, too, dear Lysander, have led a dull life.

LYSANDER: (*Patting her hand*) Your life would not be dull with me, Gladys, but I fear rather short.

GLADYS: Short, but why?

LYSANDER: (*Seriously*) It's something I cannot quite understand. (*Rising*) My love, oh my intense love, goes on and on, yet the objects change every year. (*Turning out*) Hazel and I had had a glorious year, but it all ended so miserably that night when I held her head under water in the bathtub. (*Pause*) Geraldine and I were perfectly mated our year together, but it seems it all had to come to an end that lovely moonlight night when we were standing on the balcony terrace and I pushed her over the iron railing. (*Pause*) Margaret and I were spending a blissful second honeymoon abroad when I couldn't resist the temptation to ease her off the promenade deck. And dear Gwendolyn, I can still hear those weak cries of hers from the closet . . .

GLADYS: But each had a wonderful year?

LYSANDER: A year for all years. (*Lysander sits on lounge with Gladys*)

GLADYS: One year *with* you, dear Lysander, might be worth more than the rest of a lifetime *without* you.

LYSANDER: Two of my wives said the very same thing when they married me.

GLADYS: Then they knew of this . . . this weakness of yours?

LYSANDER: Oh, yes.

GLADYS: And they married you anyway?

LYSANDER: It's all a matter of values.

GLADYS: Yes, it's all a matter of values. (*Rises, crosses right, and looks out*) You know, Lysander, I'm not supposed to see you again.

LYSANDER: But you will?

GLADYS: (*Turning*) Of course. My dear, this is a problem. I can't live without you, and I won't live long with you.

LYSANDER: (*Thinking*) Yes, it is a problem.

GLADYS: I gave my word that after you went through that door (*Pointing right*) I'd never see you again.

LYSANDER: Then I shall simply not use that door.

GLADYS: But how . . .

LYSANDER: The window. (*Rising*) Find some sheets, Gladys. We'll knot them together and out I'll go.

GLADYS: Oh, Lysander, this is why I love you so. Life would never be dull with you. Short, perhaps, but never dull.

LYSANDER: Shall I kiss you, my dear?

GLADYS: Please. (*Gladys steps left and extends hand. Lysander gallantly bows and kisses Gladys who almost swoons with ecstasy. She then goes to bureau right, takes out sheets, and hands them to Lysander*)

GLADYS: I wonder, dear Lysander, if the sheets . . . would hold *me* up also.

LYSANDER: Of course, my dear.

GLADYS: I couldn't go with you of my own free will, you know. But if I were . . . kidnapped . . . I could easily satisfy my conscience.

LYSANDER: (*Simply*) Then I shall kidnap you.

GLADYS: (*Happily*) Oh, Lysander, you are so kind! (*Both Lysander and Gladys begin knotting sheets together. Lysander ties the end of one to a solid object and throws the other end out of the window left*)

LYSANDER: (*Turning*) I'll go first, love, so I'll be under you in case anything happens.

GLADYS: I've never been kidnapped before.

LYSANDER: Exciting, isn't it?

GLADYS: The most exciting thing that has ever happened to me.

LYSANDER: Shall we leave?

GLADYS: In a moment. One last look. This was a lovely room. (*Pause*) I remember the children playing here. How long ago. Their sweet, noisy cries of laughter. And I remember other sounds. (*Walks about the room*) Edna's, when she was just six, breathing heavily, oh so heavily that night we almost lost her. And the voice of my brother the last time he visited me. Here, in this room. I never saw him alive again. Where are those voices. Where? How calm the room is. As if nothing had ever happened. As if nothing *would* ever happen. (*Pause*) Yes, this was a lovely room . . . for a lovely life. But one must go on. On and on. (*Pause. Turning left*) Do you think, dear Lysander, that *I* might be . . . an exception in this line of wives. I mean, that I might . . . live longer than the rest?

LYSANDER: M'mm, possible, my dear, but not probable.

GLADYS: It's just fate, I guess, and we can do nothing about it.

LYSANDER: One must be philosophical.

GLADYS: You don't have any sort of idea how it might happen . . . to me?

LYSANDER: I don't . . .

GLADYS: (*Quickly*) Oh, I'm not asking you to tell me, Lysander. I was just a little curious. You know how women are.

LYSANDER: Love me, dear Gladys, and trust me. Something will come to my mind.

GLADYS: Something painless, perhaps.

LYSANDER: Perhaps.

GLADYS: Dear Lysander, you are so thoughtful. But, I mustn't delay your kidnapping me.

LYSANDER: Off we go! (*Lysander hops over the sill and disappears from sight. Gladys watches him for a moment and then turns to look at the room*)

GLADYS: Goodbye, room. Goodbye, house. Goodbye, children. Oh, my dear, dear children. I wonder if they'll miss me when I'm gone.

LYSANDER: (*From below*) Mrs. Pomperoy.

GLADYS: Coming dear. (*Turning*) My, has any woman ever received such a romantic proposal? Well, at least any woman . . . living? (*Mrs. Pomperoy laughs a little, climbs over the window ledge, waves a last goodbye to audience, and disappears as the curtains close*)

THE END

THE ROCKERS

THE ROCKERS

CHARACTERS

Mrs. Thominson
Mr. Peterson
Mr. Hooper
Mrs. Kroggs
Mr. Darlell
Miss Claxton

Place: The terrace of the Blue Sea Manor, a paying home for the aged in California
Time: The present

THE ROCKERS

(The scene is on the terrace of the Blue Sea Manor, a home for those aged who have the money to provide for a semi-luxurious finale to life. Down left is a table with several chairs around it. To the right of it is a rocking chair. To the right downstage are two other rockers placed together. Against the wall, upstage right, is a dart board. Against the wall, left center stage is a table. Upon this table are placed various games, a sewing basket, a box of candy, a telephone, etc. As the scene opens we see Mr. Hooper and Mr. Peterson sitting at the downstage table on the left, playing chess. MR. HOOPER is in his late sixties, a fading relic of a once robust man. He has a reddish complexion (probably high blood pressure) and silver hair, tinged here and there with black. MR. PETERSON is a sickly looking, deaf, rather thin man, also in his sixties. A man used to overalls, his high starched collar is a constant source of irritation to him. Both men seem intent on their game and seem not to notice the lady sitting on one of the rockers downstage right. She is MRS. THOMINSON, a plain, plump, motherly-looking woman in her late sixties. She has a pencil in her hand and seems to be studying something she has written in a little black notebook she holds in her lap. After several moments have elapsed, Mr. Peterson, who has been studying the board with complete attention, suddenly cries out and makes several moves across the board, taking several of Mr. Hooper's men and placing them with his growing pile of winnings. At the sound of Mr. Peterson, Mrs. Thominson looks toward them. Her glance is noticed by Mr. Peterson who quickly turns to Mrs. Thominson)

MR. PETERSON: (*Sincerely*) Oh, I'm so sorry, Mrs. Thominson. I didn't mean to cry out like that. Hope I didn't upset anything you had in your mind. I mean about your poetry.

MRS. THOMINSON: No, that's all right. I guess I wasn't thinking about my (*Pause*) poetry, anyway.

MR. PETERSON: What's that?

MRS. THOMINSON: I just said . . .

MR. HOOPER: (*Interrupting*) Why don't you turn up your voltage!

MR. PETERSON: I'm trying to make my batteries last longer.

MR. HOOPER: If you're going to use such . . . low voltage you might as well not wear that thing at all!

MR. PETERSON: (*To Mrs. Thominson*) Hooper's mad because I made the dandiest move you just about ever saw. Took two more of his men. Reminded me of a move I made back in Minnesota with old Jud Hawkins—you know—ran the drug store in Clementville. Did I ever tell you about him? Strangest fellow you'd ever want to meet. Nice, though. Awful nice old fellow.

MR. HOOPER: How's the poem coming along, Mrs. Thominson?

MRS. THOMINSON: The poem?

MR. HOOPER: Yes, you were telling me last night this new poem was about the sea.

MRS. THOMINSON: Oh yes, (*Rather guiltily*) the sea. It's going to be called (*Beaming*) 'The Sea and I.'

MR. HOOPER: Nice title.

MRS. THOMINSON: Yes, but I have a feeling someone has already used it. Do you remember any poem about the sea called 'The Sea and I'?

MR. HOOPER: H'mm. Don't seem to remember any such title. Might have been used. Most poets seem to like writing about the sea, don't they?

MRS. THOMINSON: Oh yes, Mr. Hooper, that's because the sea is so inspi . . . rational. That's why I like Blue Sea Manor so much—because of the view. (*Stands*) Imagine just looking out as we're doing now and seeing . . . the great blue Pacific ocean. (*Looks over heads of audience*) How calm it is this morning. All those still, smooth waves stretching way, way off as far as China. It doesn't seem possible, does it? (*Half turn again to group*) And yet, do you know, there're lots of my friends back in Montana who've never seen the ocean at all, or even *been* to California!

MR. HOOPER: That so?

MRS. THOMINSON: Oh yes. Some manage to make trips,

but most of the others don't seem to have the time. Or when they have the time, they don't seem to have the money. (*Mrs. Thominson crosses to table back left and picks up sewing basket*)

MR. HOOPER: Montana's always one state I seemed to miss in my travels. Not much there, is there? (*Mrs. Thominson stands in front of table with basket in hand*)

MRS. THOMINSON: (*Quickly*) Oh yes, it's lovely in the summer time, that is, before it gets too hot. The last two weeks in May are especially lovely. The winter's over and the summer heat hasn't begun yet. And all the spring flowers still seem fresh and unwilted. Then, I always liked the last two weeks in October. It's not really cold yet, but the air is crisp, and all the leaves are turning colors. (*Stepping forward*) Red, purple, orange, and golden. That's one of our busy parts of the year because we're always trying to get things ready for the first big snow storm.

MR. HOOPER: Cold in the winter, hot in the summer. Don't think I'd like it. (*Mrs. Thominson crosses to rocker downstage right and sits down*)

MRS. THOMINSON: Oh, it's funny, Mr. Hooper, but after awhile, you don't get to notice it so much. People just seem to take it in their stride. In between blizzards in the winter, there are lots of parties at the different farms. I remember one time we went over to Mrs. Gabbie's house for Sunday dinner and didn't get back home for three weeks. (*Thoughtfully*) Awfully bad blizzard that was. (*Gaily*) But those three weeks were real enjoyable for me. We spent them making angel costumes for the Christmas pageant. (*Mr. Peterson has been alternating his attention between the chess board and Mrs. Thominson, but now speaks up*)

MR. PETERSON: I was an angel once.

MRS. THOMINSON: Really?

MR. PETERSON: A little boy angel. I didn't want to be an angel, but my Ma made me. She was teaching Sunday school at the time in the Swedish Lutheran church. They give that church a coat of fresh paint every year, whether it needs it or not! Pardon me while I turn down my voltage. No use wasting the battery just to hear me. Yep, I went to the same church all my life until the Doc said Minnesota was too cold for me. That's what he told my sons too. Too cold for me. Gotta go to California where it's warm, that's what the doctor said. Won't live another year in Minnesota, he said. I didn't pay no attention to him, but my sons, Willie and Jack, they wouldn't be satisfied 'till they packed me out here. I told them it was too expensive being in a place like this, but they said their plumbing business was doing real good and for me not to worry. (*Pause*) Sometimes I wish I'd never gone to that doctor like Willie and Jack wanted. I could be real helpful now in their plumbing store. (*There is a sympathetic pause observed by both listeners. Then Mrs. Thominson begins straightening out the tangled wool yarn of the youth's sweater she is knitting*)

MR. HOOPER: I got so I don't put much faith in doctors. My daughter brought one to our house one day, 'cause I wouldn't go down to see one. The Doc said Denver was too high for me. Gotta go to California, he says. Look at me. (*Straightens shoulders*) Can you imagine him telling me that? Captain of my football team in high school, and *almost* captain of the team in college except that Ned Barnett outweighed me seven pounds. Used to climb mountains on week-ends. (*Rises*) Oh, you should see those Colorado mountains. Most beautiful in the world. And you should climb them. Way to the top of those shimmering peaks, like I did. Then you look down on the whole world and it seems like nothing could be higher than you are, and everything seems strange, and clean, and wonderful. Climbed nearly all the big mountains but one, that was Old Breakerbus mountain. Not as high as some of the others, but a tough one. Always meant to climb it someday, but never got around to it, until it was too late. (*He sits again*)

MRS. THOMINSON: That's too bad.

MR. HOOPER: Bill Allen, he was my best friend in college, liked to climb mountains as badly as I did. He climbed Old Breakerbus clear to the top and he was fifty-five when he did it. I wanted to go with him but my daughter wouldn't let me. Said I was too old. Stick to my dart throwing she said!

MR. PETERSON: Guess you told her off when that Allen fellow got back, didn't you?

MR. HOOPER: (*After pause*) He never came back. (*Walks over and takes darts off board on back right wall*) Something happened while they were coming down. Bill and four other fellows were roped together and one of them slipped and lost his hold. There was a straight drop of over a thousand feet down to the ledge where they fell. (*Pause*) They say they've got a little rock casing there on the ledge. Glassed in, and in it they've got Bill's equipment on display with some of the other things they found. Poor Bill. Sure wish I could have been with him. Never took a pill in his life. Never one ache. Yet, I was always trim to him. Bill was lucky. He didn't have to grow old. (*There is a strained pause as all are thinking. After a moment, Mrs. Thominson speaks softly*)

MRS. THOMINSON: That's the most unpleasant part of growing old—losing old friends one by one until all seem to be gone. One makes new friends but they're never the same as the old friends who have passed on. (*Mr. Hooper, after much aiming, throws a dart at the board. He stands near the table backstage left*)

MR. HOOPER: And yet science is trying to get out a serum so people will live two hundred years.

MRS. THOMINSON: I doubt if anyone past sixty would buy any of it. (*At this moment Mrs. Kroggs breezes in. MRS. KROGGS is a fat woman in her late fifties. Her hair is obviously dyed, and her make-up is styled for a much younger woman. Her eyelashes are long and false as are her fingernails. Mrs. Kroggs, as she enters the room, poses herself dramatically in the doorway*)

MRS. KROGGS: (*Cheerfully*) Good morning, everybody! Good morning! (*Mr. Hooper continues aiming, slightly annoyed at the disturbance of Mrs. Kroggs*)

MRS. THOMINSON: Good morning. Did you sleep well?

MRS. KROGGS: I never sleep well when I sleep by myself.

(*Mrs. Kroggs ducks and walks under line of dart throwing. Mr. Hooper throws dart. Mrs. Kroggs continues speech center stage*) Oh dear, I guess I was married just too long. A woman never realizes how nice it is to have a man in bed until after her husband's gone and she's too old to get out and *hustle* up another. (*Mrs. Kroggs takes delight in saying these, what she considers a little shocking, remarks. The others are almost used to her, though, and pay slight attention to her slightly off-color comments. Sometimes, they seem grateful for the small bit of sensuousness left in her*)

MRS. THOMINSON: Oh, Mrs. Kroggs, you always make me blush so!

MRS. KROGGS: I'm sorry. (*Crosses over, sits in rocker next to Mrs. Thominson, and pats her hand affectionately*) I keep forgetting where I am and that I'm still quite new . . . *here.* I've been such a woman of the world, one might say . . . Experienced so many things. So many lovely, lovely things . . . (*This last is drawn out with a long rapturous sigh*)

MR. HOOPER: (*Pausing in his aiming*) You had only one husband, Mrs. Kroggs?

MRS. KROGGS: Yes, unfortunately, only one. But such an understanding one. A woman of my beauty and charm would *naturally* be *bombarded* with attention from other men. So natural. But Mr. Kroggs understood. (*Rising*) Beauty must be shared. That's what he always said. To him, I was a lovely flower visited by oh so many bees, for *honey* one might say. But Mr. Kroggs was always my King Bee and knew it. My sweetest honey was saved only for him. He was a dear, dear soul who had only one fault. That name! Kroggs. Ugh. No matter how you pronounce it, it still comes out Kroggs. My only solution seems to be in marrying another name. Mr. Hooper, you're nice. (*Goes to Hooper*) Why don't you marry me? Hooper. Hooper. No, that's too much like a delayed burp. Peterson, now that's a nice name. Perfectly nice. (*Crosses and faces Peterson, then turns her back to him in a Bathing Beauty pose*) Do you think I'm charming, Mr. Peterson?

MR. PETERSON: (*Blushing*) Indeed, Mrs. Kroggs, but

don't you think I'm much too old for you? (*Mrs. Kroggs is delightfully flattered at Mr. Peterson's little joke*)

MRS. KROGGS: Please call me Flossie. Did you ever notice how all fat girls seem to be called Flossie and all girls named Flossie seem to be fat? (*Begins to cross right to rocker previously occupied*) I'm sure if mother had named me . . . Amanda, I'd grown to be quite thin. Amandas *are* usually quite thin, have you noticed?

MRS. THOMINSON: Miss Springer's first name is Amanda, isn't it? (*Mrs. Kroggs sits again and pats Mrs. Thominson's hand*)

MRS. KROGGS: Oh, that poor Miss Springer. I think she's thin because she eats so little. She's behind two months in her payments here and she's afraid if she eats a lot, Mrs. George will say something to her about it. Poor dear lady, if she can't make her payments here, she'll have to go to a charity home.

MR. HOOPER: Doesn't she have any relatives or friends to write to?

MRS. KROGGS: She's utterly without relatives. Too proud to write her friends, I think. Isn't it a shame about her money? Did she say anything to any of you about it? (*The others shake their heads*)

MRS. KROGGS: Of course I'm not the one to gossip, but I heard from a source I've sworn not to mention, that the lawyer who handled her money got into some trouble and is being sent away to prison.

MRS. THOMINSON: But surely she'll be able to get some of her money back.

MRS. KROGGS: It'll take a long time. And perhaps she won't get any of it. She's expecting a letter today about her affairs. The letter will tell her definitely whether or not she has any money left.

MRS. THOMINSON: Poor Miss Springer. What'll she do if the money *is* all gone? She's never worked, has she?

MRS. KROGGS: I don't think so. Did you ever notice her hands? Like a girl's. And you know what she uses on them? You'd never guess in a million years. I was in her room one night and saw her. She uses just . . . soap and water! Can you imagine! (*Amazed*) Just soap and water!

MRS. THOMINSON: (*Turning*) Poor dear lady.

MRS. KROGGS: Oh, but let's not be glum so early in the morning. I feel *particularly* lucky today. (*Rises*) So let's begin our bridge game right away.

MR. HOOPER: But the mail hasn't come.

MRS. KROGGS: Must we always wait until after the mailman comes before we begin our bridge game? I hate routine. (*Mrs. Kroggs crosses toward table back right, ducks under Hooper's "line of fire" and bends over chocolate box, swaying her hips as she attempts a decision. Hooper pauses a moment in his dart aiming and eyes Mrs. Krogg's behind as a substitute target. Before a decision can be reached, however, Mrs. Kroggs picks up the box of chocolates, turns, ducks again under the line of fire, and takes center stage*)

MRS. KROGGS: That's what I dislike about Blue Sea Manor. No matter how you try to avoid it, everything seems to fit into some awful routine. It was different at Rocky Edge Manor in Santa Barbara. Something exciting was always happening. Of course I was younger then. The only thing I disliked about Rocky Edge Manor—I'm telling you this so you'll never make the mistake of going there—is that awful sign they have on their front lawn. And it's even on their letterheads. Guess what the sign says! (*All shake their heads*)

MRS. KROGGS: It's a big sign, with a pretty decorated border. And in big letters it says "Rocky Edge Manor." Underneath in smaller letters, but large enough for everyone to see, it says: (*Pause*) "Home for the Aged." Isn't that simply terrible. I was embarrassed when any of my friends ever came to see me there. (*All of them react sympathetically to her feelings and share them. Mrs. Kroggs gestures the box of candy to the others, but all shake their heads. Mrs. Kroggs then seats herself in rocker left stage and begins eating chocolates*)

MRS. KROGGS: Believe you me, as soon as I finished my month in advance payment, I moved away. But you know, they had the nicest young man who worked there. I forget what he was called. He had black curly hair and clear blue eyes. Supervised (*Tittering*) recreation. And do you know what some of those women said—of course I never believed it—but they said he made love to some of the guests who stayed there. Not in their rooms, but in his little cottage. It was at the back of the property, covered with vines, and there were lots of little paths going to it. It was on the same path to the little marble drinking fountain, so anyone could pretend she was going out for a drink of water, and *instead,* pay him a little visit. He was a very nice young man, though, and I'm sure the stories were all untrue, because several times I hinted to him that I often grew restless at night and walked in the garden and that it might be nice if we had chocolate or something in his cottage. But you know, he never took advantage of me.

MR. HOOPER: I'm sure it was just talk.

MRS. KROGGS: Do you think so? I almost stayed there an extra month because he was so nice. But that awful sign! (*Mrs. Thominson drops her knitting momentarily and begins to rock*)

MRS. THOMINSON: Santa Barbara is so beautiful.

MRS. KROGGS: (*Beginning to rock also, in unison with Mrs. Thominson*) Oh, I like the scenery here just as well. In fact, I just love all of California. You can't imagine how terrible I feel when I think of all those years you spent in Montana. How long and dreary they must have been.

MRS. THOMINSON: Oh, time went by very quickly back there. So many things to do.

MRS. KROGGS: My goodness yes. I've read some of those farm women work like slaves. From morning to night, working all day long. I really don't see how or why they put up with it. It's a wonder your family let you get away at all.

MR. THOMINSON: (*Stopping her rocking quickly*) Oh, I didn't want to leave.

MRS. KROGGS: You didn't!

MRS. THOMINSON: Well, not very badly. (*Beginning to rock slowly again*) After my husband died, I took turns living with my children. I have three—two boys and a girl. My oldest boy and my daughter and their families live in Minneapolis, and my youngest son has his own farm in Montana, right close to our old home farm.

MRS. KROGGS: Is that the one whose wife isn't expected to live, the one you were telling me about.

MRS. THOMINSON: Yes, that's Jimmy. His wife has been sick now for two years.

MRS. KROGGS: H'mm, it's a wonder he hasn't got you back there slaving again.

MRS. THOMINSON: Oh, he doesn't want me. I mean, all the children think Montana climate is too severe for me, so they insist I live out here.

MRS. KROGGS: Well, I should think they're right. Places like Montana may be all right for some people, but you're different. Oh, I can see you're different. (*Crosses to right rocker*) You're meant to live nicely, and write poetry, and all that. (*Hooper crosses and pulls darts from board and returns to throwing position*)

MR. PETERSON: How big is your son's farm, Mrs. Thominson?

MRS. THOMINSON: Oh, it's a nice size, six hundred acres. It has a cozy little house and a nice big barn. There's a family orchard that's real productive. The year before she took sick, Emma, that's Jimmy's wife, put up over 500 quarts of fruit.

MRS. KROGGS: No wonder she's dying.

MRS. THOMINSON: Oh, that isn't much at all. (*Picks up knitting again*) One year I put up 750 quarts.

MRS. KROGGS: You poor woman!

MRS. THOMINSON: And I only had three spoils out of the whole bunch. That was the year my pears won first prize at the County Fair. (*Drops knitting, stops rocking*) My, what a year that was. My picture in the home town paper. Right on the front page. My husband bought me a new purple hat covered with yellow daisies, just for the picture, and you know, the photographer decided I'd look better with no hat at all, but Pa, he wasn't mad about it. Next week later, I had another picture taken with the hat on and gave it to Pa. He was real pleased.

MR. PETERSON: What's that?

MR. HOOPER: Turn up that darned voltage! How many grandchildren did you say you had, Mrs. Thominson?

MRS. THOMINSON: (*Beginning to rock again*) Five. (*Stops rocking*) Poor little tikes. I wonder how they're getting along while their mother's so ill. Mrs. Griswald, that's a neighbor woman, is living at my son's farm, but I know she isn't doing things right.

MRS. KROGGS: Well, you're here in California now with the sunshine and your poetry, and don't you ever let them talk you into going back there to live. They might say it's just for a visit, but you be careful they aren't a-wanting you to come back to work like a dog for 'em again. My goodness! (*Mr. Darlell enters. DARLELL is a retired actor, distinguished looking and active for his advanced age. He is putting on a cape with sweeping gestures*)

MR. DARLELL: God ye good morrow, gentlemen. God ye good den. (*Mr. Darlell brushes off a speck of invisible dust from his cape*) Romeo and Juliet, Act II, scene 4. I never forget a role.

MRS. KROGGS: (*Rising*) Oh, good morning, dear Mr. Darlell. Isn't this going to be a glorious day?

MR. DARLELL: (*Looking out front*) Ah yes. See how the morning opes her golden gates, and takes her farewell of the glorious sun! (*Again a finger brushing*) Henry VI.

MRS. KROGGS: (*Gushing*) We'll be playing cards in just a moment, so won't you stay and join us?

MR. DARLELL: Sorry, but I'm just leaving. (*Crosses to downstage left*) Now is the sun upon the highmost hill of this day's journey. So many journeys may the sun and moon make us again count o'er ere love be done! I'm giving a reading of Hamlet this morning to some friends.

MRS. THOMINSON: Mr. Darlell, I think it would be nice if you recited Shakespeare for us some evening.

MR. DARLELL: (*Bowing deeply*) Some evening I shall, madame. Are you familiar with the immortal bard?

MRS. THOMINSON: After a fashion. I like Shakespeare because he uses so many familiar sayings. (*The nurse, Miss Clax-*

ton, enters, carrying a tray of glasses and pills. MISS CLAXTON is a hard-faced practical nurse in her early forties)

MISS CLAXTON: Good morning, everybody. (*All in room respond except Darlell*)

MRS. THOMINSON: Has the mail come?

MISS CLAXTON: Not yet.

MRS. THOMINSON: It seems to be a little late this morning. (*When Mr. Darlell sees Miss Claxton he attempts to slip away*)

MISS CLAXTON: Just a moment, Mr. Darlell. (*Darlell is now face-to-face with Miss Claxton*) You got away from me yesterday, but not today. So, two pink pills instead of one.

MR. DARLELL: You and your damned pink pills! (*Beginning to walk downstage left again*) Look everyone, Miss Claxton's really built, isn't she? (*To the men on his left*) Like a thermometer!

MISS CLAXTON: With the right person, a thermometer can raise *quite* a temperature. (*Mr. Darlell bows to her, then while Miss Claxton looks on, he places the two pills in his mouth, takes water and seems to swallow them. As soon as Miss Claxton's back is turned, however, he places his hand up to his mouth, removes the pills and puts them quickly into his coat pocket*)

MR. DARLELL: (*Turning right*) Thy wit is as quick as the greyhound's mouth; it catches. (*Miss Claxton goes from person to person, dispensing pills*)

MR. DARLELL: A sweet touch, a quick venue of wit! Snip, snap, quick and home! It rejoiceth my intellect; true wit!

MRS. KROGGS: (*Sitting in rocker right to swallow pills*) Miss Claxton, the next time you see Dr. Albright, will you ask him if I can increase my vitamin E intake. I'm sure that would make me more . . . vital! (*The men laugh, especially Mr. Darlell*)

MRS. KROGGS: What's so funny! They say vitamin E helps in raising the blood count or something. (*Darlell crosses right and stands beside Mrs. Kroggs who is delighted with his attention*)

MR. DARLELL: Comes in the sweet o' the year; for the red blood reigns in the winter's pale. Nothing can allay, nothing but blood, the blood, and the dearest valued blood. (*Darlell runs hand across Mrs. Krogg's shoulder and back which excites her greatly*) Yes, dear Mrs. Kroggs, your mind is all as youthful as your blood. But, here I'm dilly-dallying. (*Steps left*) I must be off. Goodbye, everybody. Parting is such sweet sorrow . . .

MISS CLAXTON: (*Unconsciously*) . . . that I shall say good night till it be morrow. (*Miss Claxton is embarrassed as she realizes what she has done*)

MR. DARLELL: Wench, you love me!

MISS CLAXTON: Go on, get out, and be careful, Mr. Darlell, don't you over exercise yourself.

MR. DARLELL: Miss Claxton, you have an evil mind! (*Mr. Darlell begins to leave, followed by Miss Claxton who passes him at door. As she goes, Mr. Darlell slaps her one on the behind. As soon as they are gone, Mrs. Kroggs rushes to door, watches them disappear, and then turns to the others*)

MRS. KROGGS: (*At doorway*) H'mp, saying he was going to recite Shakespeare to friends. I know where he's going. Down to that lady piano teacher's house. Mrs. Stirrup's her name. (*Coming forward*) I was out walking the other morning and I saw him going in there. And you know what, a few minutes later she pulled down the blinds in one of her rooms. 'Course I don't know what room it was, but it looked to me like where the back parlor *ought* to be.

MR. HOOPER: (*Chuckling and hitting his right knee with his hand*) Well, well, didn't know the old boy still had it in him.

MRS. KROGGS: Have you ever noticed those little packages which come in the mail to him from Los Angeles? Well, they're from some doctor and one of my friends there says this doctor is a gland specialist and that he sends out hormones to his patients all over the world.

MR. HOOPER: I wonder if he's expensive . . .

MRS. KROGGS: Oh, frightfully, he was going to charge me . . . I mean, I've heard . . . (*Sitting down weakly in rocker left*) . . . my friend says his rates are high.

MR. HOOPER: But he seems to get . . . results, judging from Mr. Darlell.

MRS. KROGGS: (*Quickly*) I really don't see what he sees in that music teacher. Why, she's skinny as a rail and blonde and all faded-like. You know the way blondes get. What any man can see in a woman like that when there are more desirable ladies around I will never know. But enough of these designing women! Dear Mrs. Thominson, how is your poetry coming? (*Mrs. Kroggs crosses over and sits next to Mrs. Thominson*)

MRS. THOMINSON: It's coming right along.

MRS. KROGGS: My, how I envy you. (*Pats Mrs. Thominson's hand*) (*Dramatically*) The gift of poetry must give a person a great amount of personal satisfaction.

MRS. THOMINSON: (*Half-heartedly*) Yes, I suppose so.

MRS. KROGGS: (*To others*) And isn't it *wonderful* that she has time now to compose instead of spending all of her time on one of those awful Montana farms. Oh, I *shudder* when I think of it. Not a moment for one's self.

MRS. THOMINSON: (*Thoughtfully*) Perhaps it's better that way sometimes.

MRS. KROGGS: Have you finished your sea poem yet?

MRS. THOMINSON: I've finished the first draft. Of course, I'll probably change it later. (*Rather guiltily*) It's in free verse.

MR. PETERSON: Why don't you read it to us, Mrs. Thominson. I'm sure we'd all enjoy hearing it. (*The others agree verbally*)

MRS. THOMINSON: It's called 'The Sea and I'. I'm worried about the title, though, because I have a feeling it's been used before.

MRS. KROGGS: Oh, I wouldn't worry.

MRS. THOMINSON: I try not to.

MRS. KROGGS: Just a minute, dearie, I must have a chocolate with this. (*Mrs. Kroggs crosses left, takes chocolates from seat and sits in rocking chair left. After taking a chocolate, she poises it in air and smiles for Mrs. Thominson to begin*)

MRS. THOMINSON: Well, here goes. (*Stands*) 'The Sea and I . . .

MR. PETERSON: (*Interrupting*) Just a moment, Mrs. Thominson. This is worth turning up my voltage for.

MRS. THOMINSON: (*Repeating*) 'The Sea and I'.

So azure the sea, a mirror to the sky,
Azure and brooding, the sea and I.

Sometimes peaceful, then stormy, always sly,
Azure and brooding, the sea and I.

Snow-capped waves, tossed low, tossed high,
Azure and brooding, the sea and I.

Endless, eternal, a scream and a sigh,
Azure and brooding, the sea and I.

(*To deliver this poem, Mrs. Thominson looks out over the audience, occasionally turning to her friends as she recites. However, as the poem progresses, she seems to forget her friends and concentrates entirely on putting her "all" into the poem's delivery. The others in the room listen blank-faced, their mouths dropping at the phrase 'a scream and a sigh'. Mrs. Thominson ends her poem with her voice in the air, as if it were a question. She then stands motionless. The others in the room are also motionless. After a moment, Mrs. Thominson turns to them, rather meekly. Still blank-faced, Mrs. Kroggs looks at Hooper who looks at Peterson who looks back at Mrs. Kroggs. Mrs. Kroggs smiles, says something nice and is joined in this by the others. Mrs. Thominson, pleased, begins to sit in her rocker again. Miss Claxton now enters, carrying the mail*)

MISS CLAXTON: Here's the mail, everybody. (*They all pretend to be casual about the mail, but all betray an intense eagerness*)

MISS CLAXTON: Card for Mr. Peterson, from Minnesota. Letter for Mrs. Thominson from Montana. And I guess that's all that's here.

MRS. KROGGS: The other letter?

MISS CLAXTON: It's for Miss Springer. Air mail, special delivery, so guess it's important. (*Miss Claxton exits*)

MRS. KROGGS: I was expecting a little box today from Los Angeles.

MRS. THOMINSON: You were?

MRS. KROGGS: Just more (*Flustered*) chocolates, but it seems more exciting to get them by mail, don't you think? (*Mr. Peterson turns to Mr. Hooper*)

MR. PETERSON: I can read this later, Hooper. We've got an exciting game to finish.

MR. HOOPER: No, go on and read it, Peterson. You wouldn't have your mind on your game with a letter from home in your pocket. (*Mr. Peterson begins reading card and Mrs. Thominson turns to Mrs. Kroggs*)

MRS. THOMINSON: Come, sit over here by me, Mrs. Kroggs, and we'll see how everything is at home in Montana. (*Mrs. Kroggs almost eagerly joins Mrs. Thominson to share her letter*)

MRS. KROGGS: I'm certainly anxious to hear about your son's wife. I'm afraid that pneumonia will set in and you know what happens. This younger generation just can't take what us oldsters can. I mean, what the older people can take. (*Mrs. Thominson opens her letter and begins reading to herself*)

MRS. THOMINSON: Oh, it's very bad news, Mrs. Kroggs.

MRS. KROGGS: She's dead?

MRS. THOMINSON: No. But she's taken a turn for the worse and Jimmy says the doctor thinks she might not pull through it.

MRS. KROGGS: Oh, I'm so sorry. (*Mr. Peterson has finished his card, put it away, and begins again his game with Mr. Hooper who has seated himself again at the table*)

MRS. THOMINSON: That's about all in the letter except that Jimmy says I'm not to worry, and I'm to enjoy myself out here in California. And that everything is going fine and that Mrs. Griswald is taking care of things and that I'm not to worry at all about anything.

MRS. KROGGS: That son of yours sounds real nice. It's not every son who treats his mother so nicely. Anything else in the letter?

MRS. THOMINSON: No, that's all.

MRS. KROGGS: I thought from the way the letter started, it was your son wanting you to come back and live on the farm and take care of things. My, wouldn't that be awful. Milking, doing the cooking and washing and ironing, and all that fruit to can. And three children besides.

MRS. THOMINSON: Yes, there's a lot of work to be done on a farm. (*Mrs. Kroggs suddenly sees something off right. She gets up and goes to window, peering through edge of the curtain*)

MRS. KROGGS: Why look, there's Miss Springer.

MR. PETERSON: Where? (*Both Mr. Peterson and Mr. Hooper stand*)

MRS. KROGGS: Going out the back way, with a suitcase in her hand.

MR. HOOPER: It must have been bad news she got in the letter and she couldn't bear to face us.

MRS. THOMINSON: Poor Miss Springer, I do hope she makes out all right.

MRS. KROGGS: (*Glancing at watch in an attempt to find excuse to change unpleasant subject*) My goodness, it's almost eleven, and we haven't *started* our bridge game. Let's see. How shall we partner off? Last time Mrs. Thominson and I played Mr. Hooper and Mr. Peterson. Suppose this morning Mr. Hooper and I play partners against Mrs. Thominson and Mr. Peterson.

MR. HOOPER: That's O.K. with me. Although I think we'll be taking unfair advantage of our opponents.

MR. PETERSON: Don't you fool yourself, Hooper. I can be a mighty sharp card player when I choose to be.

MR. HOOPER: You may be able to lick me at chess, Pete, but when it comes to cards, that's my field. (*Mrs. Kroggs brings out card table from behind table left back, which Mr. Hooper gallantly takes from her and erects*)

MRS. KROGGS: Oh, thank you, Mr. Hooper, it's so nice to have a strong man around to help the weaker sex. (*The others draw up chairs. Peterson sits, and Mrs. Kroggs hands the cards from off the table to Mr. Hooper*)

MR. HOOPER: What shall we play this morning?

MRS. KROGGS: Oh, anything.

MR. HOOPER: Ever played Black Ace?

MRS. KROGGS: Why no, I don't believe I've even ever heard of it.

MRS. THOMINSON: Is it a new game?

MR. HOOPER: No, it's an old game I read about once in some book. The game is played once a month only. All the cards are dealt out. Whoever gets the ace of hearts is *murdered* by the person getting the ace of spades. Quite an exciting game they say.

MRS. THOMINSON: My, we couldn't play that game very often.

MR. HOOPER: The world is full of people.

MRS. KROGGS: I'll play the game if you promise I don't get any aces at all! (*The group laughs, then the telephone on the table right back rings. Mr. Hooper answers it*)

MR. HOOPER: Hello? Yes, Mrs. Thominson, yes . . . she's here. Just a minute. For you, Mrs. Thominson. Western Union, a telegram . . . (*Mrs. Thominson almost stumbles out of her chair as she rushes to the telephone. Mrs. Kroggs sits down and joins the others in staring frankly at Mrs. Thominson and listening to the conversation*)

MRS. THOMINSON: Hello, yes, this is Mrs. Thominson. Yes, could you wait just a minute? (*To Mr. Hooper*) Mr. Hooper, I wonder if you could write this down—it's a wire from Montana. (*Hooper quickly takes out a pencil and the back of an envelope. He stands prepared to write as Mrs. Thominson turns back to the telephone*) All right, operator. Slowly, so my friend can write it down. "Emma passed away this morning. Mrs. Griswald will try to take care of things. Letter follows. Love, Jimmy." Yes, operator, I have it. Was that all? Yes, thank you. (*Mrs. Thominson slowly hangs up the telephone, and turns to the others*)

MRS. THOMINSON: Poor dear Emma.

MRS. KROGGS: (*Softly*) Perhaps it's for the best, being sick so long.

MRS. THOMINSON: She was such a dear, dear girl. Poor Jimmy, how miserable he must be. (*Mrs. Thominson takes a few steps aimlessly about the room as the others watch her intently*) How did the wire read, Mr. Hooper?

MR. HOOPER: (*Reading*) Emma passed away . . .

MRS. THOMINSON: Just the last part, please.

MR. HOOPER: Mrs. Griswald will try to take care of things. Letter follows.

MRS. THOMINSON: (*Sitting in rocking chair down right*) That's a strange sentence. Mrs. Griswald will try to take care of things. I wonder if Jimmy's trying to tell me something. Try to take care. I'll bet he means that everything she does is done poorly, not the way I'd do things.

MRS. KROGGS: It is worded in a peculiar way.

MRS. THOMINSON: (*Thinking*) I'm out here in California just because Jimmy's worried about my health. But people aren't healthy when they're not happy . . .

MR. HOOPER: I'd venture to say he'd like to have you back there.

MRS. THOMINSON: (*Quickly*) Do you think so! Oh, if it were only true.

MR. PETERSON: But, on account of the snow and everything, he's afraid of your health.

MRS. THOMINSON: My health to the dickens! Oh, pardon me, that's the first time in my life I've ever sworn, but I'm so het up!

MR. HOOPER: If you want to go, Mrs. Thominson, let nothing on earth stop you.

MRS. THOMINSON: Nothing will. (*Rising*) There's a train leaving for Montana this morning. Oh, I've memorized that schedule by heart. What time is it now?

MRS. KROGGS: 11:15.

MRS. THOMINSON: There'll be a streetcar coming by at 11:23 which arrives at 11:32. The Montana train leaves at 11:34 giving me two minutes for my ticket. I can make it!

MRS. KROGGS: But, my dear, you've your packing . . . (*Mrs. Kroggs rises*)

MRS. THOMINSON: I've never ever unpacked. My goodness, I can't stand here like this. I've got things to do. (*Turns to go*) You don't think I could be wrong . . . about the wording?

MR. HOOPER: I think your son's calling you, Mrs. Thominson. (*Mrs. Thominson rushes to doorway, then stops and turns*)

MRS. THOMINSON: God bless you. All! (*Mrs. Thominson exits. The others are quiet for a moment*)

MR. HOOPER: I guess we can start our bridge game now. Three handed.

MRS. KROGGS: Shall we play auction or contract?

MR. PETERSON: Let's play contract. I'm better at it.

MRS. KROGGS: (*Standing behind her chair*) Wouldn't it be nice if we could interest Mr. Darlell in card playing. I'm sure he does too much running around for a man his age. (*Pauses, wistfully*) My, I wish I could teach something and have my own little studio. (*Sits*)

MR. HOOPER: Who wants to deal?

MRS. KROGGS: You, Mr. Hooper. You deal the best of all and I always get such good cards when you're giving them out. (*Mrs. Kroggs suddenly sees something through the left window and rises*)

MRS. KROGGS: Why, there's Mrs. Thominson running down the front steps with both of her suitcases. My goodness, you'd think she was escaping from a prison or something.

MR. PETERSON: Look, she's forgotten her little book of poetry.

MR. HOOPER: (*Getting up from chair and stepping out right*) I'll mail it to her, 'though I imagine she's lost all interest in poetry. Mrs. Thominson is a woman who thinks . . . just keeping things going . . . lots more important than writing pretty poems.

MRS. KROGGS: (*After a pause*) Here comes the streetcar . . . (*Hooper turns left*) There, he's stopping for her.

MR. HOOPER: She's made it . . great old girl!

MRS. KROGGS: (*Sincerely*) Off to that wonderful farm of hers, with her cooking, and her canning, and her grandchildren. (*They are quiet for a moment*)

MR. PETERSON: (*Softly*) Isn't it wonderful . . .

MRS. KROGGS: (*Softly*) . . . to be needed.

(*The curtains close slowly*)

THE END

DEATH CELL

DEATH CELL

CHARACTERS

JIM, A boy in his twenties
MRS. ANDERSON, His mother
JAILER
CHAPLAIN

Place: A death cell
Time: The present

DEATH CELL

(The scene takes place in a dimly lighted cell. Only one flat need be used—the back flat showing the barred opening. Jim and his mother sit at a table. JIM is in his middle twenties and is dressed in khaki. MRS. ANDERSON is in her fifties and wears a simply-cut gray cotton dress. Both are rather grim and cold-faced. Throughout the play one senses a feeling of embarrassment in their last meeting together. After the curtains open there is a moment of quiet, then Jim draws on his cigarette slowly. A jailer passes. Jim calls out softly to him.)

JIM: Oh, Jailer. (*The jailer stops and looks into the cell*)

JIM: How much time? (*The jailer steps back and looks at his watch*)

JAILER: Just six minutes more.

JIM: Thanks. (*The jailer looks at him for a moment, then goes on*)

MRS. ANDERSON: Did he say six minutes, Son?

JIM: Yeah, Ma. (*Both Jim and his mother are silent again for a moment*)

JIM: Ain't it funny, Ma, how when you got a lot to say to a person and there ain't much time, that nothing seems to come out at all.

MRS. ANDERSON: I know, Son.

JIM: Just like the summer I spent at Grandma's when I was a kid. Remember that, Ma? And remember Grandma calling you long distance in the city so's I could talk to you? Grandma and I had planned just what I was going to tell you. How I'd gathered eggs in the morning and helped Grandpa rake in the newly mown hay. I was going to tell you how beautiful that hay was—shining golden in the sunlight. Then, there was the mill pond. I was going to tell you how in the afternoons the kids met there for a swim in the cool green water. And how, when there weren't no girls around, we stripped off suits because it felt so good to be free of everything. Free to dive and swim in the pond or to stand on the big old stump and let the meadow air sweep by us, being as free as the air itself. Oh, I had a lot of things to tell you, Ma, but when I heard your voice I forgot everything except how beautiful you were and how I wanted to be home with you. Then the operator said our time was up, but I said "I love you, Mother" real quick-like before she cut us off. Do you remember that, Ma?

MRS. ANDERSON: Yes, I remember, Son. That's all I wanted to hear. (*Again there is silence*)

JIM: I still love you, Ma. Very much. Even after . . . I'll go on loving you. I want you to remember that. You'll feel it close to you all the time no matter where you are. Love's that way, Ma. Nothing can stop it. Even death's no barrier.

MRS. ANDERSON: I wish . . .

JIM: (*Quickly*) Don't think, Ma. About anything. Just feel and remember. Remember me always saying you've been the best mom a boy ever had. Everything was just wonderful—the two of us together, until Life stepped in and smashed everything. Life in the form of George Cradshaw.

MRS. ANDERSON: Don't think of it, Son.

JIM: How can I help thinking? I'm glad he's dead. Do you hear, Ma, I'm glad he's dead. He deserved to die. Someone should have killed him before . . . long before he started ruining so many helpless people.

MRS. ANDERSON: Yes, he was a wicked man, but it's God who must decide who's to live or to die. That's not for us humans to decide. Who knows, Jim, perhaps all this just had to be. Think on it a bit. There are some who say God guides our every action whether it be good or bad.

JIM: Do you think so, Ma?

MRS. ANDERSON: Yes, and that makes this . . . this hour easier to bear.

JIM: If I'd only known when we met Cradshaw how things would have turned out. The mess he got us in. The Hell and misery.

MRS. ANDERSON: Please, Jim. There's nothing anyone can do now.

JIM: I was sure the governor would come through with a reprieve. Sure, a man died. But he asked for it. No one was sorry to see him die. No one at all. Surely the governor. . . .

MRS. ANDERSON: Don't torment yourself like this. The governor's sent his final word.

JIM: Maybe he'll change his mind before . . .

MRS. ANDERSON: Put little hope on earthly things, my son. Our only hope lies . . . beyond. You believe that, Jim, don't you?

JIM: I believe, Ma. There sure ain't no hope here on earth.

MRS. ANDERSON: Don't be bitter, Son. Smile a bit so I can take that smile away with me and remember it always. There's good in the world and there's bad. A little of both is mixed in everyone of us. It's just luck and fate what brings out more of one or the other. That's all. God knows how it is. He must know. He made us. (*Again there is a short silence*)

JIM: Do you want me to click on the lights, Ma?

MRS. ANDERSON: No, Son, I like it this way. It makes it easier to see the past. The past with you always in it. The full, happy past they can never take away. Memories of our little house on Hickory Street. Of you when you were young. (*Again there is a silence. The jailer passes again and looks in*)

JIM: Oh, Jailer, got an extra cigarette? Guess I've used up all mine. (*The jailer takes out a pack and hands it to Jim*)

JAILER: Keep the pack.

JIM: Thanks, but a couple'll do. (*Jim takes out a couple cigarettes and hands the pack back to the jailer*)

JAILER: Anything else? (*Jim looks towards his mother, then back towards the jailer*)

JIM: No, I guess not. Thanks. (*Again the jailer turns to go, but Jim catches his attention with a gesture. Jim then forms a sentence on his lips and says it silently. The jailer looks down at his watch and then raises two fingers up for Jim to see. The jailer goes away*)

MRS. ANDERSON: He seems to be a very nice man.

JIM: The jailer? Oh, yeah.

MRS. ANDERSON: And the chaplain. He was nice too.

JIM: Yeah.

MRS. ANDERSON: You'll see him again before . . .

JIM: Sure.

MRS. ANDERSON: It's almost time, isn't it, Jim?

JIM: Yeah, Ma. (*Silence again*)

MRS ANDERSON: I wonder what kind of people live on Grandma's farm now? I hope it's a young couple with children. Grandma's farm was such a nice place for children. I'll never forget the wonderful times I had there. When I was a child. Grandma had the most wonderful attic. Did you ever go up into her attic?

JIM: One time, Ma, when it was raining. The gang went up and we told ghost stories. Some of them just about scared me to death. . . . I remember a story one of the girls told. Don't remember her name. Think it was Jeannie or something. She got just to the part where there were footsteps on the stairway and sure enough we could hear footsteps just like she was a-saying. Jeannie must have heard them too, 'cause she stopped, but the footsteps didn't. They kept getting louder and louder until finally they stopped at the attic door. When the door slowly opened some of the girls screamed. And do you know what it was, Ma? It was Grandma! She'd made some cookies and brought a whole tray of them up with glasses of apple cider. Grandma was wonderful. How can those kind of people ever die, Ma. I know they live on, somehow.

MRS. ANDERSON: Do you think so, Jim?

JIM: Else, why . . . why anything? If we just die, then there's no meaning to anything. And that's not true. There's meaning everywhere. There's meaning when the skies grow cloudy and rain falls for the hungry earth. There's meaning when the trees drop their leaves in autumn, seem dead through the winter, then blossom out in the spring. That's the wonderful thing about spring, Ma, ain't it? Everything is fresh and new. Like giving the leaves a fresh start.

MRS. ANDERSON: That's strange.

JIM: What, Ma?

MRS. ANDERSON: It's autumn now. Outside the trees are dropping their leaves. Soon they'll seem dead. But they won't be, will they, Jim? Spring will come. It may take a long time. It may seem never to come. But it will. And with new life. (*The chaplain appears outside the cell door. Both mother and son see him. The chaplain looks in for a moment, then turns his head slightly*)

MRS. ANDERSON: I guess I have to leave you now, Jim. Goodbye. (*Mrs. Anderson takes Jim's hand and kisses him on the forehead*)

MRS. ANDERSON: God bless you, my son.

JIM: Goodbye, Ma. Remember the trees. Don't never forget 'em. (*The chaplain takes Mrs. Anderson by the hand and they disappear. Jim stands a moment looking after them. Then he sits at the table. After a moment, he gets up, lights a cigarette, and paces a bit. Finally, sensing a presence, he turns and waits for the chaplain to appear at the door. The chaplain pauses, then steps into the room*)

CHAPLAIN: Strengthen yourself, my son.

JIM: Is it . . . Chaplain . . . is it . . .

CHAPLAIN: Yes, it's . . . all over. Done quickly as possible. You can claim the body if you like.

JIM: That's why I've waited. (*The chaplain takes Jim by the arm and they slowly leave the cell as the curtains close*)

THE END

FEAR

FEAR

CHARACTERS

MRS. GREEN
BILL EDWARDS

Place: A back bedroom
Time: The present

FEAR

(The scene is a back bedroom of a well-furnished middle class home. There is a doorway leading into the room from back right. At extreme back right there is a closet. The door to the hallway must be closed in order to enter closet. Downstage right there is a table, being used as a desk, and a chair. Center stage, with its head against the back wall is a large "Hollywood" style bed (no footboard.) Rear left stage, against the wall, is a chest of drawers. Center left is a window and upstage left is seen an armchair and lamp. As the curtains part we notice an opened newspaper on the unmade bed. After a moment Mrs. Green enters. MRS. GREEN is a small dark woman in her sixties. She has a small mouth and large, expressive eyes. Mrs. Green is simply dressed in a gray woolen dress. The woman is followed into the room by a young man who calls himself Bill Edwards. EDWARDS is in his middle twenties, a clean-cut fellow of taller than average height and seems a little underweight. He is sandy-haired and has gray eyes. Today he wears brown slacks, white shirt with no tie, and a leather jacket cut along military lines. There is something about Edwards which causes one to like him at first meeting)

MRS. GREEN: (*Entering*) As you see, I haven't had time to tidy-up. The last roomer, Mr. Grimple, just left this afternoon.

EDWARDS: It seems a nice room.

MRS. GREEN: Oh, I'm sure you'll find it so. That is, if you take it. It's the only room I rent out. Mr. Grimple was here two years. He was transferred by his company to Chicago. (*Mrs. Green notices that the window left is closed. She crosses over and opens it*)

MRS. GREEN: There's always a nice fresh breeze coming through the back part of the house. Even in summertime. We used to have a big old pepper tree outside which cut off some of the breeze, but my husband chopped it down just before he died. Three years ago. (*Thoughtfully*). It was pleasant to sit under the tree in the summertime. (*Pause*) I think it's a nice room and you'll find it quiet here.

EDWARDS: Yes, it is quiet. Quiet as a graveyard between funerals. (*Mrs. Green is stopped for a moment by his speech. Edwards crosses over, inspects chair left front and sits in it. Mrs. Green crosses right and continues her speech*)

MRS. GREEN: The room has complete privacy. It can't be seen from the streets. And the buildings on both sides of the house are used for offices now, so there's no one there in the evenings to make a lot of noise.

EDWARDS: It's a little island.

MRS. GREEN: Yes, my husband liked it that way. But after he died, I found it *too* quiet and isolated sometimes. That's why I rent out this room. You see, I've always been afraid of living alone. Isn't that silly?

EDWARDS: Not very, with all these murders. (*Indicating paper on bed*) Is that the morning paper?

MRS. GREEN: It must be. Mr. Grimple always subscribed to the Herald. (*Edwards crosses and picks up paper*)

EDWARDS: Still in the headlines.

MRS. GREEN: About the murders?

EDWARDS: Yes. How would they sell newspapers if there were no killings? (*Reading*) "Police are still baffled by the wave of murders which is sweeping over the university area; however, in connection with the Rose Pennoyer murder. . . ."

MRS. GREEN: Poor Mrs. Pennoyer!

EDWARDS: Did you know her?

MRS. GREEN: She lived in the next block. We used to meet at the corner market sometimes, and during the war we were both on the same block committee. Imagine anyone wanting to kill her. Why, she wouldn't want to harm a fly. I personally think there's a madman loose. Didn't steal a thing, choked her to death like he did the others.

EDWARDS: (*Still reading*) Well!

MRS. GREEN: What is it? Another murder?

EDWARDS: They've found the killer's fingerprints! On the

doorknob at Mrs. Pennoyers'. The police believe he's left-handed. First clue they've managed to find.

MRS. GREEN: Left-handed. Speaking of clues, I've thought of going to the police and telling them what I know about Mrs. Pennoyer. I mean about something she said. But I suppose they would just laugh and I can't bear to have people laugh at me.

EDWARDS: I wish you'd tell me. I have kind of a special interest in these murder cases. (*Mrs. Green sits at table right*)

MRS. GREEN: Well, last Tuesday, the very day she was killed, we met in the market, Mrs. Pennoyer and I. She told me her last roomer—she kept a roomer, too. In fact, all the women killed kept rooms, isn't that strange? Well, anyway, Mrs. Pennoyer's last roomer was an old man who died on her and she told me that she wasn't going to rent out the room again to anyone except a very young man. Perhaps one going to the university.

EDWARDS: That is a clue!

MRS. GREEN: (*Standing*) But this isn't showing you the room. If you're through with the paper, I'll take it down with me when I clean. (*Edwards hands her the paper in his left hand. It drops to the floor. Edwards picks it up with his left hand and hands it out to Mrs. Green again. Mrs. Green stares for a moment at the extended hand, then takes the paper mechanically*)

MRS. GREEN: I change the linen twice a week. There's a half-bath next door with a shower. This room also has a nice large closet. There, behind the door. (*Edwards crosses to back right. Mrs. Green crosses left*)

MRS. GREEN: (*Apologetically*) The door to the hallway has to be closed before you can open the closet door. It's really no trouble because I imagine you'll want the hall doorway closed most of the time. That is, if you take the room. (*Edwards looks at Mrs. Green for a moment, then slowly closes the door to the hall. A hint of fear is seen on Mrs. Green's face. Edwards slowly opens the closet door and looks in*)

MRS. GREEN: You'll notice that the closet is lined with that special moth proof paper. It's just as good as moth balls and it will keep your clothes from having that offensive smell. (*Edwards disappears into the closet. Mrs. Green seems nervous, goes left and glances quickly at the newspaper in her hand. She holds it down, however, when Edwards re-enters the room*)

EDWARDS: It's a fine deep closet. Tomb-size. (*Edwards closes the closet door and turns to Mrs. Green who still stands on the opposite side of the room*)

EDWARDS: Do you have a key for this door?

MRS. GREEN: No, but there's that bolt. My husband put bolts on all the doors because I was always so afraid. Noises frighten me terribly. Especially strange noises. That's another reason my husband cut down the pepper tree. It was getting so large that its branches would scrape on the rooftop. You can't imagine what a weird sound it made. Sometimes I was sick with fear, even knowing that it was just that old tree clawing at the shingles. (*Edwards turns toward the bolt on the hallway door and with a quick movement closes the bolt. Mrs. Green again shows sign of fear*)

MRS. GREEN: It's never been bolted before. There's been no one who wanted to close it.

EDWARDS: *I* wanted to.

MRS. GREEN: You must be an awfully strong man, Mr. . . .? I don't believe you gave your name.

EDWARDS: No, I'm not strong, except in my fingers. They're Cyclopean sinews of steel. (*Edwards holds his hands out in front of him and looks at them*)

EDWARDS: I guess I could do anything with them. Anything at all. When I was a kid I broke some of my right fingers playing baseball, but there's never been anything wrong with my . . . left hand. (*Mrs. Green attempts to laugh, a little foolishly, nodding toward the door*)

MRS. GREEN: I hope you'll be able to open that bolt. Wouldn't it be amusing if we were locked in here. Trapped.

EDWARDS: Trapped? Yes, this room is like a trap, isn't it? Your hallways are like twisting gopher holes, each leading to this back room where some omnipotent being has set a trap to catch whatever stumbles into it.

MRS. GREEN: It's getting a little warm in here. Mr. Grimple complained sometimes that it was too hot. Perhaps you've noticed it too, the heat. Have you? (*No answer*) Maybe you wouldn't want the room, especially during the summer. Mrs. Abbley across the street has a front room for rent, I believe. Front rooms are always much nicer. Much more cheerful. Of course, if you should open the door again, there's a little breeze. (*Edwards turns toward the bolt and places his hand on it. Then he turns toward Mrs. Green again*)

EDWARDS: And if I can't get it open?

MRS. GREEN: I could go to the window and cry for help.

EDWARDS: Would anyone hear you? The offices next door have closed and all the employees gone home. Would Mrs. Abbley across the street hear you?

MRS. GREEN: I don't know. That's why I've always disliked this location. If something should ever happen, there'd be no one. . . .

EDWARDS: Yes?

MRS. GREEN: It's so hot in this room, isn't it? I believe I should be ill if I had to live here. Mr. Grimple was ill a great deal of the time. I'm sure that . . . (*Edwards suddenly unbolts the door, but doesn't open it*)

MRS. GREEN: Oh, I'm so relieved. Isn't that my telephone ringing downstairs?

EDWARDS: No. No telephone rang. It's so quiet here that I would have heard it.

MRS. GREEN: Yes, it is quiet. Too quiet, Mr. Grimple always said. Sometimes the quiet can be really annoying. Perhaps you wouldn't like it at all. Yes, the room is hot and things are always too quiet.

EDWARDS: The doctors told me to find some place quiet. I'm just out of a hospital. They were so crowded they let some of us leave if we promised to find quiet places to live.

MRS. GREEN: You should find a place in the country then. I'm afraid you won't find any place in the city as quiet as a hospital.

EDWARDS: (*Angrily*) Hospitals! (*Coming forward*) What

makes you think hospitals are quiet! On the contrary, they're very noisy. The grinding noises of hypodermic needles being sharpened. Of ice being crushed for the ice bags. Have you ever heard the crushing of ice? Like fragile little skulls gritted under monster hammers. And then there's the noise, the terrible squeaking noise leather makes when they're strapping someone in.

MRS. GREEN: My, that seems like a strange hospital.

EDWARDS: Strange? Yes, I suppose so. A cold white cave with the doctors and nurses appearing and disappearing as phantom objects. Unreal creatures who have no voices but whispers. And their whispers are always as the whisper of the dying wind which ushers in a smudgy night, eerie and sterile of moonlight. (*Pause*) It's getting dark outside. I see you have lights in the room.

MRS. GREEN: Yes, but Mr. Grimple said one of the bulbs was almost burned out. I'll go downstairs and get a new one to put in. If you'll just open the door.

EDWARDS: (*Quickly*) No, don't leave. Don't bother now. Besides, I think I prefer a dull light. I don't know why. In some ways I seem different from ordinary people. It's been that way ever since the war. Sometimes I feel so . . . strange. I must *seem* strange sometimes. I guess that's why girls are afraid to go out with me. They're afraid because I'm strange sometimes. (*Clicks on the light*) Why, this light isn't dull at all. In fact it's too bright. Dazzling. It hurts my eyes. But that's all right. It's quiet here. I like it. It's a back room, quiet and hidden. Veiled solitude. Away from everything and everybody. Quiet, with no one to bother. (*Edwards quickly snaps off the light and Mrs. Green gasps. Edwards snaps them on again*)

EDWARDS: Just testing. (*Again Edwards snaps off the lights and begins to whistle*)

MRS. GREEN: Please turn on the lights. It's dark now. The lights need to be on. (*Edwards continues to whistle*)

EDWARDS: Do you know why I whistle?

MRS. GREEN: The lights, please.

EDWARDS: I whistle because it is dark and I am afraid. Do you whistle in the dark, Mrs. Green.

MRS. GREEN: I've never been able to whistle.

EDWARDS: Then, what do you do when you're afraid? (*Mrs. Green doesn't answer, but one can see in the dark that she is shaking with fear. Edwards begins to whistle again, then stops suddenly*)

EDWARDS: It must be horrible not to be able to whistle when one is afraid. Whistling is a sharp-edged knife which cuts away fear layer after layer. You must learn to whistle, Mrs. Green. (*Suddenly Edwards snaps on the lights and starts rapidly toward downstage. Mrs. Green automatically steps back against the left wall*)

EDWARDS: (*Brightly*) Yes, I like it here. I'll take the room. I'll stay tonight and bring down my luggage in the morning. The doctors will be happy when I tell them about my quiet little back room. (*Edwards sits down at the table right front, takes out a check book and begins to write in it with his left hand, whistling all the while. Then he stops and looks up*)

EDWARDS: But we haven't settled about the price, have we? Checks are such demanding creatures. Demanding and curious. Their lips ask me for the rental price. (*Mrs. Green has edged over to the bed and gauged the distance between herself and the door, when suddenly Edwards turns and faces her squarely*)

EDWARDS: Tell me what you're thinking. Your price, Mrs. Green. (*Mrs. Green steps back and seems to be attempting to brave herself*)

MRS. GREEN: I'm sorry but I can't let you have the room.

EDWARDS: (*Surprised*) What!

MRS. GREEN: I've just remembered my brother is coming out from Chicago. I'll need the room. I don't know how long he'll be here. Perhaps if you come back.

EDWARDS: (*Standing*) The sign, Mrs. Green. You had the sign out. Room for Rent. Back room and quiet. That's what it said, Mrs. Green. Room for Rent.

MRS. GREEN: I'm sorry. I'm sure they'll be glad to take you across the street.

EDWARDS: It's a front room across the street, Mrs. Green, and there are other roomers. Here it is a back room and you live alone. All alone. And it is quiet. No one close to bother or to notice what happens here.

MRS. GREEN: Please, go, won't you? I'm expecting a friend and I must prepare dinner.

EDWARDS: (*Stepping toward her*) You're like the rest. You think I'm strange.

MRS. GREEN: No, it isn't that. It's my brother—coming from Detroit. . . . No, Chicago!

EDWARDS: I'm not well, Mrs. Green. I know that. I'm afraid I shall be ill again. Do you know what it is to be afraid, Mrs. Green? I fear because my mind fears. Fears and knows not what it fears. Black fear pierced sometimes with the green lightning of sickness.

MRS. GREEN: Please go! (*Mrs. Green is almost weeping with controlled hysteria. Edwards looks at her for a moment, then looks down at his hands*)

EDWARDS: (*Almost to himself*) So strong. (*Edwards drops his hands and slowly starts for the door. At the door he turns*)

EDWARDS: (*Almost friendly*) Perhaps I can come back sometime.

MRS. GREEN: Yes, do. Come back and see if the room is empty. I'm so sorry. About everything.

EDWARDS: Sorry? Yes, so am I. Sorry. (*Edwards looks at her one last moment, then goes out. As soon as he leaves, Mrs. Green almost races to the door, closes it quietly, and attempts to bolt it, but she is unsuccessful. She throws her back against the door and holds it until she hears a door slam downstairs. At the sound her body slumps a bit, then she looks at the newspaper in her hands and begins to cry. After a moment, she almost drags her body over to the bed and sits down, the newspaper in her lap. After a moment, she takes out her handkerchief and begins to wipe her eyes. Her body is still shaking and she begins to laugh with her crying, all done rather silently. There is a new look of relief on her face and she looks up, attempting to find courage when we see the hallway door slowly open. Edwards steps slowly inside and looks toward Mrs. Green who hasn't heard him. Edwards slowly raises his hands to a clutching position and begins to gleam savagely at Mrs. Green as the curtains close)*

THE END

THE MOMENT

THE MOMENT

CHARACTERS

George Sampson, A wealthy man
Barstow, A lawyer
William Halstead, A bankrupt

SCENE:

A small office (*Possibly library-office in private home*)

THE MOMENT

(The scene opens with Barstow sitting behind table center stage looking through some papers in his brief case which rests on the table. Sampson looks out window right. SAMPSON is a small-boned wiry sort of man. BARSTOW is a nondescript)

BARSTOW: I have the check here, Mr. Sampson. Do you still wish to leave it as a signed blank check?

SAMPSON: Yes. (*Turning left*) I want the pleasure of handing it to William Halstead and telling him to fill in the amount. All these years I've rehearsed this moment. Yes, after all these years the moment has finally come. You know, Barstow, very few people on this earth ever realize the height of their dreams. As a lawyer, *you* know it's usually the *opposite* in most people's lives.

BARSTOW: Yes, unfortunately.

SAMPSON: At first I'd planned to refuse William Halstead the money when he came to me. Let the factory fail. But after thinking it over I decided it'd be better for me to help him save it, then always be in the background to remind him of his saviour. (*Stepping left*) You never knew my wife, the *first* Mrs. Sampson, did you, Barstow?

BARSTOW: I don't believe I had the pleasure, sir.

SAMPSON: It was no pleasure, believe me. All she had was money. (*Turning right*) She died two years after our marriage which was certainly a piece of good luck.

BARSTOW: Yes, sir. (*After awkward silence*) Have you known this Mr. Halstead long, sir?

SAMPSON: Long? (*Crosses left in front of table*) I've known William Halstead all my life, and *even longer* it seems. My father worked as superintendent of the factory under William Halstead's father. Bill Halstead and I grew up together. (*Samp-*

son walks further left and takes three darts off board stage left) The boss' son and the son of the superintendent. (*Steps right*) Went to the same schools, even the same college.

BARSTOW: You must have been close friends. (*Sampson takes a step right*)

SAMPSON: (*Quietly*) I hated him. (*Turns left and throws a dart into the board*) I hated him because I knew I was as good as he was, even if my father was only superintendent and his the owner of the town's largest factory. Things were always so *smooth* for him. But now it's to be different. The shoe's to be on the other foot. At last! This is the moment I've waited for. (*Sampson smiles savagely and throws second dart into board*)

BARSTOW: Is it true the banks will loan no more money to Halstead?

SAMPSON: Yes, it's true . . . and wonderful! There's no one to help him now except me. Me, George Sampson, the son of his father's superintendent. There's no more Halstead money in the bank. After five generations, the Halstead house up on the hill has been sold, and the factory faces bankruptcy. Yes, the Halstead line has finally run out. Started back before the Revolution.

BARSTOW: It's good of you, sir, to help Mr. Halstead like this.

SAMPSON: Good? (*Smiling bitterly*) I've not done a good thing in all my life. I make no pretenses, Barstow. My only ambition has been to acquire money, and with money, power. It hasn't been easy, but now everything will be realized.

BARSTOW: How could you have known about the Halstead misfortune so far in advance?

SAMPSON: Because I know William Halstead. (*Crosses right behind the table*) He's more interested in . . . music than in business. Artists can't run factories. In college, Halstead took a business course, but he spent most of his time with the college glee club, arranging songs and all that bosh. It was easy for Halstead, just as everything was easy. I think that's why I hate him so much. What time is it, Barstow?

BARSTOW: (*Looking at watch*) Three minutes until ten.

SAMPSON: Three more minutes. Just three minutes and the moment will be here. William Halstead will walk through that door. (*Pointing right*) *Not* the fine, proud William Halstead, last of the line, but a broken bankrupt. In his forties, a disastrous failure. He'll come in. I'll ask him to sit down. I'll do no speaking at first, just let him sit there and think of his failure. I'll play cat and mouse with him. Let him know that I'm uncertain of his ability to bring the factory out of its debt. Then, when I've given him about enough, I'll take out the check and toss it across the table. Perhaps it will fall on the floor. Yes, that would be nice. He'd have to reach over and pick it up. Give me the check, Barstow, I want to see how I should toss it. (*Barstow hands the check to Sampson. Sampson tosses it across the table, then retrieves it*)

SAMPSON: I suppose you think I'm a . . . little mad, Barstow. Perhaps. But its a *glorious* madness. All my life has been but a preparation for this moment. After today nothing else matters. Nothing at all, Barstow. I'll be free. Free for the first time in my life. No more compulsion of duty or purpose. After this moment, it will all be over.

BARSTOW: (*Rising*) Excuse me, sir, but I believe I hear footsteps.

SAMPSON: Halstead! (*Sampson crosses left in front of table. He looks at the dart in his hand, starts to raise it to throwing position, but changes his mind, smiles, and places it on the table. Barstow steps to the left of his chair. Both men watch doorway right. Soon William Halstead enters. HALSTEAD is a handsome man in his early forties. His body is tired and sags a little, but there is a small smile on his face, and a glint in his eyes which suggests a newly-found happiness. When Halstead enters, Sampson smirks just a little, but attempts to control his happiness. He motions for Halstead to occupy the chair at his desk. Halstead does so. Sampson waits for Halstead to speak, but Halstead doesn't*)

SAMPSON: This is Mr. Barstow, Bill. My attorney. (*Halstead nods in a friendly fashion, then begins looking about the room. Barstow crosses right and sits down in chair right, pretending to be occupied with papers*)

SAMPSON: You've made a last trip to the bank? (*Halstead nods*)

SAMPSON: (*Attempting not to betray his eagerness*) Any luck? (*Halstead looks at him for a moment, then shakes his head slowly. Sampson straightens a little with relief*)

SAMPSON: I understand Phyllis has left you. (*Halstead looks up for a moment, then nods*)

SAMPSON: Wives can be a great comfort sometimes in periods of distress. (*Halstead nods again. Sampson is becoming a little exasperated. He's not enjoying this as much as he'd planned*)

SAMPSON: My attorney has drawn up some papers, Bill. That is, in case I *decide* to lend you the money. Everyone has advised me against it. Throwing good money after bad. But money isn't everything, is it, Bill? There're other things. (*Turning out*) Honor. Tradition.

HALSTEAD: You've been a good friend, George. One of my best. And your father was my father's closest friend. They had so much in common. Strength. Purpose. Courage.

SAMPSON: About the money.

HALSTEAD: I'm glad they're not alive. This moment would have hurt them terribly. Perhaps *your* father more than mine.

SAMPSON: (*Irritated*) I've decided to advance the money, Halstead.

HALSTEAD: (*Not seeming to hear*) Ah, those were wonderful days, George. The past. Remember the days up at the lake. (*Looking out*) You and I, and our fathers. Walking 'long the bank's edge. . . You and I, spinning pebbles across the quiet blue water. And at college. Each new day more exciting than the last. One's youth always does seem happy after it has passed.

SAMPSON: Mr. Barstow has arranged the papers. All the details are in order.

HALSTEAD: My happiest moments at college were with the choral groups. I got such a kick out of helping them. Putting notes wherever I wanted and waiting and watching for the effect.

The college had a fine choral group. Still does. They tour now every year. Did you know that, George?

SAMPSON: (*To Barstow*) If you'll get out the papers, we can begin. (*Barstow crosses behind table and hands Sampson some papers. He then resumes his seat at chair right, pretending to be occupied with other papers*)

HALSTEAD: I've often wondered if one can ever regain the exhiliration one has in youth. Can one ever shake off the burdens of adulthood and responsibility?

SAMPSON: I even have the check, Bill. Just tell me the amount and I'll fill it in. I've a pen here somewhere. (*Sampson takes pen out of coat pocket*)

HALSTEAD: You're really wonderful, George. This gesture of yours means a great deal to me. Old ties *are* the strongest. I know you have little faith in me and for that you're justified. Yet, you're willing to help this way. You're a fine man, George Sampson.

SAMPSON: (*Stepping right*) The amount, Bill.

HALSTEAD: The directors tell me it'll take seventy-five thousand to restore our credit ratings. (*Sampson steps right to table and hastily writes in the figure. He then hands the check to Halstead, being careful to see that it isn't dropped. Halstead takes the check, looks at it for a moment, then slowly tears it in half. The gesture cuts Sampson like a knife. Sampson steps back*)

SAMPSON: My God, what are you doing?

HALSTEAD: (*Rather sadly*) It's . . . all . . . over, George. The past is dead. The glory, tradition, all dead. (*Happily*) And I'm glad.

SAMPSON: Glad? What are you raving about!

HALSTEAD: If I took your money it would be only a matter of time until I'd need your help again.

SAMPSON: That doesn't matter, Bill. I've more than enough money. I'll double the amount on a new check. (*Sampson takes his check book out of pocket. Halstead, however, holds up his hand slowly. Sampson stops his movement*)

HALSTEAD: I'm calling it quits.

SAMPSON: But you can't do this, Bill. . . .

HALSTEAD: The directors suggested to me that the plant be incorporated. There are ten who will take care of the financial backing.

SAMPSON: You're letting the factory go?

HALSTEAD: They're giving me ten per cent ownership.

SAMPSON: (*Turning left in disgust*) Ten per cent!

HALSTEAD: It's more than I deserve.

SAMPSON: But the factory. It's always been owned by the Halsteads. Have you no pride. No sense of decency. Letting it pass to your . . . employ*ees!* (*Halstead puts up a hand again*)

HALSTEAD: It's all come to an end, George. And what a relief. I met with the directors before coming here. What a glorious moment it was. (*Picks up dart subconsciously and rises to his feet*) And what a glorious new feeling I have. For the first time I'll be able to live. To live. To breathe as a free man.

SAMPSON: Ridiculous! The Halsteads are factory owners. What else . . .

HALSTEAD: I'm accompanying the college singing group on its tour, making new arrangements, helping out in whatever way I can. After the tour, I don't know . . . But I do know I'll be free to do whatever I like. Free of purpose, free of compulsion. Oh, it's a glorious feeling, George. (*Juggling dart in hand*) You should feel it yourself some time. (*Places dart on right side of table*) Well, I've got to leave. The train's off in an hour and I've a little packing to do. (*Halstead turns and exits right in front of table with a brisk step. Sampson, still in shock, stands dazed. After a moment, he walks slowly over to behind the table and looks out*)

SAMPSON: (*Softly*) He's done it again. (*Sampson then, in a slow, cold rage, sits in chair. Almost subconsciously, he picks up the dart he had placed on the table, closes it in his fist, and begins beating the table with his fist as the curtains close*)

THE END

THE HUNTER

THE HUNTER

CHARACTERS

EMO: A Nebraska sugar beet farmer in his late forties.
MAUDE: Emo's wife. In her early twenties.
MRS. BLAXTON: Maude's mother, who has lived with her daughter and son-in-law since Maude's marriage to Emo almost two years ago.

Time: The present.
Hour: Late evening.

THE HUNTER

(As the curtains part we see the interior of a Nebraska beet farm kitchen. It is noticeably bleak with only the faded red gingham curtains at the window offering relief from the sordid dullness. At the back there is a double screen doorway leading to the outside porch and back yard. Besides the door is a nail hook upon which is hanging a cheap, cotton coat. On the left side of the stage there are two doors leading into other parts of the house. Also on the left side, against the wall, is an old, much-used stove. Off center left, downstage, is a kitchen table, upon which are sugar bowl, salt and pepper shakers, and a various assortment of condiments. There are three chairs placed at the table. On the right downstage is an ironing board with a chair beside it holding a basket of freshly dampened clothes. The room is lighted by a naked light bulb hanging down over the table. MRS. BLAXTON is sitting by herself at the table, her back to the stove. She is in her middle fifties and is a coarse, ordinary woman. She is too thin, has a gray complexion, and pinched features. Her yellowish-gray hair is arranged in small, tight curls which cling to her head. At this moment she is wearing a soiled house dress of plain design and without sleeves. Unclean old tennis shoes are to be seen upon her stockingless feet. Mrs. Blaxton has spent most of her working years in cheap restaurants and laundries—and looks it. As the play opens she is seen in deep absorption over a copy of TRUE ROMANCE Magazine which she holds in her hands. After a moment she notices her coffee cup is empty. Putting her magazine down for a moment she slouches over to the stove, pours herself some fresh coffee, returns to the table, and again picks up her magazine. Maude now enters through back right door. MAUDE is the only daughter of Mrs. Blaxton and is in her early twenties. She is dressed in a crisp, clean, red cotton print dress, with low-cut breast lines and a short skirt. She is without stockings, but wears shiny, black pumps which match her shiny black belt. Maude is an average-sized brunette, a little too boney in her facial features to be called beautiful. As Maude enters, she seems to be in an almost breathless condition and her face is flushed.)

MAUDE: (*To Mrs. Blaxton*) Where is he, Ma? Where's Emo? Where is he?

MRS. BLAXTON: (*Still sipping coffee*) Emo?

MAUDE: Yes, Emo! Is he here in the house or did he go outside? (*As an answer to her daughter's questioning, Mrs. Blaxton simply shrugs her shoulders and turns back to her reading. Maude turns quickly from her mother and silently approaches the door at back left. After peering through it carefully she passes the stove and opens the up left door carefully, and peers into the room. As she does this, Mrs. Blaxton's curiosity is aroused and she turns her attention upon her daughter.*)

MRS. BLAXTON: (*Loudly*) What'sa matter?

MAUDE: (*With fingers to lips*) Shh!

MRS. BLAXTON: Don' you be a-shushing your ma!

MAUDE: (*Demanding*) Did ya see Emo go out the house this evening?

MRS. BLAXTON: (*Indifferently*) And supposin' I did. Can't your husband go out if'n he's a mind-to? (*Maude begins wringing her hands and crosses in front of her mother to the downstage center.*)

MRS. BLAXTON: What's wrong, Maude! I can tell somethin's wrong 'tween you and Emo. You ain't quarreled with him again, have ya? Don't fergit what I told ya about fightin' with Emo. He's made ya a good husband and it ain't likely you'll git another fine place like this for'n your living.

MAUDE: (*Bitterly*) For *your* living, don't you mean?

MRS. BLAXTON None yer lip! I do mor'n nuff for my keep here. Now, fess up, what's the trouble. It's somethin' to do with Emo, now ain't it?

MAUDE: No. Well, no and yes.

MRS. BLAXTON: What kinda talk is that?

MAUDE: It's about . . . me . . . me and Harry. There I've sed it.

MRS. BLAXTON: Harry? Who's Harry? (*Rises*) And whad ya mean Harry and you?

MAUDE: I . . . I knew you'd find out sooner or later, so here it is. I was with Harry this evening out behind the barn. Harry's a beet hand who works here. He's young and I think I love him. *(Mrs. Blaxton slowly gets up from her chair and circles behind the table towards Maude. As Maude talks she moves towards the left)*

MAUDE: *(Continuing)* Tonight, just a few minutes ago, I think someone saw us 'hind the barn together. I don' know if it was Emo or not. I don't know who it was. *(By this time Mrs. Blaxton has approached Maude from the right. A brief moment passes as she looks upon her daughter with wretched, utter contempt. Then, she strikes Maude with such force that she stumbles back against the chair and falls to the floor)*

MRS. BLAXTON: *(In white heat)* Is this what I've raised ya to be? A common little whore! What about me? Oh, I don't care what happens to *you*. But what about me? Think I can go back to that stinkin' laundry and work the rest of my life? Now you've ruined it for us both. Here I git you out of the laundry by marryin' ya to Emo. And I git you a home, didn' I? You've been a damned lucky girl to git a home like this, 'specially with a fine man like Emo who'd take your old mother in, too.

MAUDE: *(Rising to her feet)* But I don't love Emo. I never have.

MRS. BLAXTON: Love! I'll teach ya what love is! *(Mrs. Blaxton again prepares to strike her daughter, but the motion stops in mid-air as she seems to hear something)*

MRS. BLAXTON: *(Quickly)* Git up. Someon's a-comin'! Git over there *(points to ironing board)* and preten' you're working. And if he asks you anything, play dumb and lie to 'im. You always were a good liar. *(Crosses to stove)* Harry! I thought you sed it was a heifer you were so much interested in out in the barn. No good, damned two-legged heifer, that's what it was! *(Emo enters. He is a Nebraska sugar beet farmer in his late forties, over six feet tall and weighing over 200 pounds. Emo has short, black curly hair which is mingled with gray. He isn't a talkative man. In fact, he's rather cold, bitter, and very methodical. He is dressed in a faded plaid shirt, brown work pants, scuffed boots, and a vest. When Emo first enters the room, there seems to be a tense blankness about him. After glancing at his wife for a moment, he walks to the center of the room and just stands for a moment, as if in a deep ponder. In her speeches to Emo, Mrs. Blaxton displays conspicuous sweetness and consideration. Throughout the rest of the play it is obvious that Mrs. Blaxton is prepared to sacrifice anything— even her daughter— in the interest of her own security on the farm with Emo*)

MRS. BLAXTON: (*Turning*) Oh, hello Emo. Won't you have some coffee. I made a fresh pot jist so's you'd have some. I know how you like fresh coffee and ya always sed nobody could make coffee like me. (*Emo still remains silent and stares in front of him. Maude continues her ironing, not knowing whether to speak or not*)

MRS. BLAXTON: (*Pouring coffee into cup which is on table*) And do ya know what, Emo, tomorrow for lunch I'm having pork chops with that fav'rite chili sauce of yours. It's hard to fix, Emo, but of course I enjoy fixing things for you, Emo. I always have, Emo. You know that, don't ya? (*Pushes cup on table a little towards Emo*) In fact, Emo, I've never enjoyed myself so much before. Not that work's enjoyable, but of course I know you appreciate my cooking and the way I work around here for ya. It's not every mother who has sich a good home, I always say. (*Pushes cup a little more*) Ya know, Emo, I always think of ya as my son and I want ya to think of me as your mother. (*Pushes cup a little more*) And for supper tomorrow night I thought I'd fix fried chicken again with all the trimmings. Ya know, Emo, I've fixed a little book for myself showing all your fav'rite recipes. My goodness, seems like I've got so many, it'll take me a couple years or more to go through the book so's I can start back at the beginning again. (*Mrs. Blaxton picks up the cup of coffee off the table, walks over, and offers it to Emo. Emo doesn't take the cup, but crosses to downstage left and exits through door. A moment passes, then Maude steps out from behind her ironing board.*)

MAUDE: (*Whispering*) He acted so strange, Ma. Do you think he was the one? Maybe it was one t'other hands just prowling around. Or maybe it was jest our 'magination.

MRS. BLAXTON: He's acting strange-like, but not like he was mad or nothing!

MAUDE: He always does act strange. That's why I hate him!

MRS. BLAXTON: (*Quickly*) Shut up! We've got a good home here, and don't fergit it!

MAUDE: (*Sullenly*) You've got a good home. You don't have ta sleep with him. (*A clicking noise is heard from off left and Mrs. Blaxton rushes back to the stove. A moment later, Emo re-enters, carrying his leather jacket and a rifle. Maude gasps a little when she sees the gun, but Mrs. Blaxton pretends not to notice anything special*)

MRS. BLAXTON: (*Sweetly*) I'm about ready to take my apple pies out of the oven, Emo. Ya know how ya love my apple pies. Best in the county, ya say. (*Steps over to table*) Why Emo, you ain't a-goin' out again s'late? (*Emo leans the rifle against the table, then begins putting on his jacket*)

MAUDE: (*Coming forward*) Don't go out again, Emo. It's sa late. Besides, I gits lonely in the evenings. (*The above last sentence is said with almost repulsion by Maude*)

EMO: (*Slowly*) Do ya?

MRS. BLAXTON: And I've got some fresh cheese to go with the pies, Emo. My, I can just taste that pie now in my mouth. Can't you, too, Emo? (*Emo reaches over for the rifle*) And Maude can git us some fresh milk. Please, Emo, don't go out again tonight. It's gittin' so cold and I'm afraid you'll catch the flu again. It makes me feel so bad when you're sick, Emo. (*Emo glares at Mrs. Blaxton*) But of course I just love takin' care of ya. Makin' ya broths and special juices. (*Emo finishes putting on his coat, picks up rifle and heads for the back door. Maude comes up to him as he turns to go*)

MAUDE: (*Throatily*) Where ya going, Emo? It's so late. I worry when you're out late. Honest I do.

EMO: (*Softly*) I'm jes' goin' huntin'.

MRS. BLAXTON: But it's so late, Emo. It can wait until tomorrow. I'm so afraid ya'll git sick agin. 'Sides, Emo, what's there to hunt tonight? It's so dark out.

MAUDE: Ma's right, Emo. What's there to hunt at night?

EMO: (*Softly, after pause*) Skunk. (*Emo leaves the two*

women and exits out upstage right door. Both women are speechless for a moment)

MAUDE: Oh, Ma, whadya suppose he meant?

MRS. BLAXTON: It's that Harry he's goin' after. I've warned you time and again that someday you'd cross Emo, and then you'd be sorry. Skunk, huh. Well, I guess he's right. (*Maude starts for the porch door*)

MAUDE: I've got to warn Harry. (*Mrs. Blaxton crosses and stops Maude*)

MRS. BLAXTON: (*Shrilly*) Don't be a fool, Maude. Maybe it's the four-legged varmint he's after and not the two-legged kind.

MAUDE: But what if he kills Harry?

MRS. BLAXTON: Mighty good riddance if'n he did.

MAUDE. How can you say that. You don' even know Harry.

MRS. BLAXTON: No, but I know life. Sit down, Maude, and listen to me . . . listen like you've never listened to a body before. (*Maude sits slowly on the right table chair, while her mother moves over to downstage center. In Mrs. Blaxton's next speeches, we see glimpses of a tender and pitiful woman.*)

MRS. BLAXTON: Yes, Maude, I know life. Sometimes it can be sweet and beautiful, and sometimes it can be downright miserable. Most of the time it's the miserable way for most folks. Oh, I ain't got no kick a-coming, I guess, but eighteen years in a cheap, cut-rate laundry, being kicked around, gittin' starvin' wages for it, well, that ain't my idea of a good time. Can't you see it my way, Maude?

MAUDE: Why should I see it your way? I want to live my own life . . . with Harry.

MRS. BLAXTON: You're still young and healthy. It's natural ya don' think of things like this now. But wait 'til you're old and you ain't got no money set by 'cause you never made enough above makin' ends meet. Then's when you begin to think about security. That's what all old folks is a-worried about. Sometimes they fret and stew so much about it that their minds go a little off. I'm gettin' old, Maude. That's all I want from life—security. And I've got it here on the farm. We've got it here. Oh, Maude,

I admit I ain't done everythin' by you like a mother should, but I jest ain't had the time nor money. Then ya met Emo and married him.

MAUDE: Yeah, I married him.

MRS. BLAXTON: Life's changed for me, Maude. And for you, too, I can see that. Jest them two years at the laundry was beginning to work on ya. And then Emo married ya and took us away from the city to out here on the farm. I like it here, Maude, I always wanted to live in the country.

MAUDE: I hate the country!

MRS. BLAXTON: So, can't ya be nice to Emo, just for me? I ain't gonna live too much longer, so I won't always be a-botherin' and pesterin' ya like this. Besides, Emo ain't so bad. Course he's not like those romance men ya read in the magazines about. But nobody real's like that. It's jist in stories, Maude. Men are all alike—one bad way or another, and ya jist got to put up with it.

MAUDE: Harry's different.

MRS. BLAXTON: When men are young they cover up all their thoughts and bad things. But after they git married, they jist don't care no more. Then, it's jist Hell for all concerned. Now, when Emo comes back in, play up with him. And be nice to him tonight in bed. Extra nice. And case he says anything about Harry and ya—mind you don't bring it up, but in case he does, tell 'im Harry caught ya by surprise and he forced ya to kiss him. Then, tomorrow early, I'll see Harry, and tell 'im to get packin' quick.

MAUDE: (*Weakly*) But, Ma. . . . (*A sound of two rifle shots is heard*)

MRS. BLAXTON: *His* rifle. (*Both women are stunned, but Maude quickly runs to the window. Mrs. Blaxton stands by the ironing board*)

MAUDE: (*Straining*) It's so dark out, I can't see a thing. Oh Ma, do ya suppose. . . .

MRS. BLAXTON: (*Coldly*) Emo sed he was a-goin' skunk huntin'. Reckon he got what he was a-after. Emo's a good shot with that rifle of his. (*Maude breaks out into tears as she stands by the window*)

MRS. BLAXTON: (*Ordering*) Come back and sit down, Maude. Don't let Emo see ya a-cryin' when he comes back in.

MAUDE: But maybe it was Harry he shot.

MRS. BLAXTON: Then it was good riddance, I say. Jist a beet-hand, Maude. Had no business messin' with ya in the first place.

MAUDE: (*Sitting down*) It was Harry he shot. I know it. And if'n he'd kill Harry, then maybe he'd kill me, too.

MRS. BLAXTON: Crazy talk! You're his wife. Remember what I sed. Be all sugar and honey when he comes back. Men fall for that. They all do and Emo's no different. For God's sake, Maude, think of me. What'll we do if Emo kicks us out? What'll happen to me?

MAUDE: (*Starting to rise*) I can't stand it any longer, Ma. If'n it's Harry was shot, maybe he's hurt, or dying'. I've got to go to him. It's my fault, more'n his.

MRS. BLAXTON: (*Ordering*) Sit down. Shh, he's comin', I think. (*Emo re-enters, but gives no evidence to the women who wait for him to speak*)

MAUDE: (*Rising*) We heard shots, Emo. . . .

MRS. BLAXTON: (*Blandly*) Did ye have luck, Emo?

EMO: (*To Maude*) The varmint's out there on the back grass. Dead. (*Maude gasps slightly, but doesn't move. Emo crosses downstage left, stopping just as he reaches the door to his room*)

EMO: (*Simply and almost with affection*) Put on your coat, Maude.

MAUDE: My coat?

EMO: Yes, I'm goin' out again and I want ya to come with me.

MAUDE: (*Terrified*) But it's so late!

EMO: We'll leave as soon as I gits more shells.

MRS. BLAXTON: You're not goin' huntin' agin, are you, Emo?

EMO: (*Matter-of-factly*) Seems that pest had a partner. (*Emo disappears into the side room*)

MAUDE: Partner! (*Rushes to mother*) Oh, Ma, he's goin' to kill me, I know he is. Just like he killed Harry.

MRS. BLAXTON: (*Sternly*) Be quiet, he'll hear ya! It was a skunk he killed, ya heard him.

MAUDE: Come with me, Ma, I'm so afraid. I've never been so afraid before in all my life.

MRS. BLAXTON: (*Pointing*) Why don' ya look outside now, quick-like, 'fore he comes out. (*Maude, as if in a daze, follows her mother's pointing to the door, slowly takes her thin, cotton coat off its hanger, and slowly exits through the door. Mrs. Blaxton lingers a moment near the door, then slowly walks to downstage center. There is a moment's silence, then the sound of Maude's laughing which builds up to a crescendo where it breaks into sobbing. Except for tense hand and facial pantomime, Mrs. Blaxton stands unmoved until Emo re-enters*)

EMO: Where's Maude?

MRS. BLAXTON: She went ahead, Emo. (*Mrs. Blaxton crosses over to left in front of table*)

MRS. BLAXTON: I'll be keepin' the coffee hot, Emo. Tonight and every night. We git along fine together, Emo. We always will. And ya can always be sure of me, Emo. I'll always be here to fix your victuals and take care of ya. (*Emo begins to exit through the door upstage right. He is again carrying his rifle*)

MRS. BLAXTON: Remember, Emo, I'll keep the coffee hot. And there'll be pie when you git back. Hot apple pie with cold cheese. (*Emo turns back to look at her before he makes his final exit. There is no sign of emotion on his face. After he leaves, Mrs. Blaxton walks slowly to center stage. She stops when she hears a single rifle shot. Her arms go to her throat automatically and then fall limply to her side. She then sits down slowly again at the table and stares at the audience*)

(*Slowly*)

MRS. BLAXTON: Hot apple pie . . . cold cheese. . . . (*Slow curtain and. . . . The End*)

SURPRISE IN SHANGHAI

SURPRISE IN SHANGHAI

CHARACTERS

MADAME HEGGLESPOON, An elderly woman
SOPHIE HIGGENBOTTOM, A young orphan girl
HENRY SIMSTROM, An American correspondent
SINK LEE, A Chinese bellhop

Place: A street in Shanghai; later a hotel room
Time: The present or the past

SURPRISE IN SHANGHAI

(The lights of the auditorium grow dim and after a moment we see Madame Hegglespoon and her ward, Sophie Higgenbottom enter from the right. They start across the apron of the stage which represents a street in Shanghai. MADAME HEGGLE-SPOON is in her late fifties, a buxom and good-natured woman. SOPHIE HIGGENBOTTOM is a shy, timid, frank, and open-faced creature. After a moment Madame Hegglespoon stops walking and points to something she sees)

MADAME: There it is, Sophie. There's the hotel where he's staying. Hotel Metropole. That's where all these American correspondents stay when they come to Shanghaii.

SOPHIE: Please, Madame Hegglespoon, I'm too afraid to go in.

MADAME: Nonsense! You have nothing whatever to fear. Just keep your purpose in mind and you'll forget all about being afraid.

SOPHIE: But a strange man!

MADAME: All men are strange, whether you know them or not.

SOPHIE: Couldn't you come in with me, just at first I mean?

MADAME, I'd like to, Sophie, but I'm late already in seeing Father Regan and then there's the Christian Ladies League Winter Tea this afternoon. You know the orphanage depends a lot on the contributions from the Christian Ladies League.

SOPHIE: But to go up to a strange man's room and ask for money!

MADAME: It's for a worthy purpose, my dear, remember that. He'll probably be very happy to help us with a check. He's an American and Americans are all very wealthy and sentimental. They also drink a lot so it's easier to get money from them.

SOPHIE: But what'll I say?

MADAME: Just be brief and to the point. Tell him the girls' orphanage needs money very badly because of rising costs. Tell him the good work I and the other ladies are doing. Work on his emotions a bit.

SOPHIE: But Madame Hegglespoon, is that honest?

MADAME: The cause is honest, that's all that matters.

SOPHIE: But what if he says No.

MADAME: He won't.

SOPHIE: How do you know?

MADAME: Because you're young and very attractive.

SOPHIE: What does that have to do with it?

MADAME: How old are you, my dear?

SOPHIE: Eighteen.

MADAME: (*Shaking head*) You've led too sheltered a life. Haven't you ever read any of those books the girls keep hidden under their mattresses?

SOPHIE: Oh, no!

MADAME: H'mm. Dear me. Well, I can't go on wasting time like this. My friend at the hotel says the correspondent's name is Mr. Simstrom and he's to arrive at five o'clock. (*Looking at watch*) Heavens, it's ten after five all ready. You must hurry. He's to be in room eleven upstairs. Can you remember all I've told you?

SOPHIE: (*Beginning*) He arrives at five o'clock. . . .

MADAME: That's not important. Remember his name is Simstrom; he's an American; he's in room eleven; and get all the money you can from him for the orphanage.

SOPHIE: Oh, Madame Hegglespoon, I can't. I simply can't. I *did* read some of those books the girls keep under their mattresses! (*Sophie breaks out into loud sobbing*)

MADAME: Oh, for goodness sake, Sophie, I don't know why I brought you along instead of one of the other girls. Yes, I do. You're prettier than the rest. Now, dry your eyes quickly, pinch your cheeks, bite your lips, and hurry up to that man's room before anyone else from the other charities beats you to it. (*Madame Hegglespoon scurries off right, leaving Sophie alone.*

Sophie pinches her cheeks and bites her lips automatically, then marches off left with a dazed frightened look on her face. After a moment the curtains part showing a bedroom interior of the Hotel Metropole. It is a typical room of a side-street Oriental hotel which specializes in catering to foreign business men. There is a bed down left. To the right is a table and a rocking chair. After the curtains have parted for a moment, Sink Lee enters, carrying two suitcases. SINK LEE is a young Chinese bellhop who speaks tolerably good English, and who, as all bellhops, is eager to fulfill all of his guest's desires. Sink Lee is followed by Henry Simstrom, the American correspondent. SIMSTROM is not the Hollywood version of a correspondent, but one readily accepts his humor and friendliness as substitutes for any possible lack of dash)

SINK: Room eleven, Mr. Simstrom.

SIMSTROM: Just put the bags down anywhere. I'll unpack them later, myself.

SINK: O.K. I come up later and help you unpack. Sink Lee honest boy. He no steal while unpacking. He do anything else for Mr. Simstrom, but he no steal.

SIMSTROM: You have an honest face.

SINK: Oh, thank you, Mr. Simstrom.

SIMSTROM: That's why I think I'll do my own unpacking.

SINK: Oh, you make joke. Velly funny. (*Sink laughs*)

SINK: Sink unpacks for you and press out your suits.

SIMSTROM: You're just full of service, aren't you?

SINK: This hotel famous for service. That is why all the Americans, they come *here*. Not the tourists, but the others. The businessmen, the writers. . . .

SIMSTROM: Well, come by in the morning. I'm going to bed now and I don't want to be disturbed.

SINK: So early?

SIMSTROM: I've got a big day tomorrow. 'Sides, I'm tired. Is there any water in the room?

SINK: Oh, yes, in the bowl, Mr. Simstrom. Before you come, I bring in fresh water and fresh towels. The bathroom is at the end of the hall.

SIMSTROM: Yeah, I noticed. It's always *easy* to find the bathroom in these Chinese hotels!

SINK: (*Laughingly*) You make big joke again. You velly clever. (*Simstrom throws himself on bed*)

SIMSTROM: (*Almost to himself*) It'll be good sleeping on a big comfortable bed again. Well, at least a bed.

SINK: I go now, Mr. Simstrom. You tell boss I good to you, yes?

SIMSTROM: Yes. (*Simstrom tosses him a coin which Sink catches and immediately deposits*)

SINK: Thank you, sir. I see you get especially good girl tonight.

SIMSTROM: (*Sleepily*) What?

SINK: I see you get best girl in house tonight. That is possible because you go to bed earlier than the rest of the Americans.

SIMSTROM: I don't want any woman. I just want some sleep.

SINK: You no want woman? You sleep alone? By yourself? In Shanghaii?

SIMSTROM: Yes, I often sleep alone. Breaks the monotony, you know.

SINK (*Laughing*) You alla time joke. I like you.

SIMSTROM: And I like you. We're old buddy-buddies. Now, get out and let me sleep.

SINK: The girl, she come up in five minutes.

SIMSTROM: I said. . . .

SINK: There is no extra charge, Mr. Simstrom. It comes with the bill.

SIMSTROM: Get out.

SINK: You no want girl to sleep with? Nights awfully cold in Shanghaii. No heating after ten o'clock.

SIMSTROM: Maybe tomorrow night. But tonight I'm too tired.

SINK: You will have to speak with Mister Wong. He is boss.

SIMSTROM: Speak to him about what?

SINK: Sleeping by yourself. He will tell you there is no price off from your room. And the girl for this room she no gets paid, then what you say?

SIMSTROM: What in the devil are you jabbering about?

SINK: If you no want girl, then girl no get money for tonight from Mister Wong. Wong gets suspicious, may kick girl out from hotel because you no like her.

SIMSTROM: But I've never seen the girl.

SINK: All the same to Wong. He want his guests to be pleased so they stay and pay their bills.

SIMSTROM: O.K., send the girl up. And tell her to bring her knitting. She can sit here for awhile, then leave.

SINK: That no good, Mister Simstrom. Girls no lie to Wong. They tell on you.

SIMSTROM: Oh, God!

SINK: I send very best one to you, Mr. Simstrom. You no want poor girl to lose job?

SIMSTROM: O.K., tell her to come up, but if she snores, out she goes, job or no job.

SINK: She no snore. I know! (*Sink laughs mischievously, then leaves. After a moment Simstrom begins shaking his head and laughing softly to himself. He takes off his coat and loosens his tie. Then, after taking off his shoes, he throws himself flat on the bed, back to the door. After a moment there is a feeble knock. At first Simstrom doesn't hear. The knocking is heard again, still feeble but louder*)

SIMSTROM: Not already? (*Sighing*) Come in. (*Simstrom still lies on his bed, with his back to the door. The room is now in semi-darkness. The door opens and in walks Sophie. There is a frightened look in her eyes, but a resolute expression on her face*)

SOPHIE: (*Weakly*) Mr. Simstrom?

SIMSTROM: Yeah, close the door and take off your things. (*Simstrom still has his back to Sophie. Sophie closes the door and then takes off her hat*)

SIMSTROM: Maybe you'd better close the shutters first. (*Sophie doesn't understand, but she is so eager to please that she does so without questioning*)

SIMSTROM: You, whatever your name is, do you speak English?

SOPHIE: Oh, yes sir.

SIMSTROM: I'll tell you from the start that it wasn't my idea that you come up here.

SOPHIE: Oh, yes sir, I know.

SIMSTROM: You don't have to stay all night. Just long enough so you can leave without being noticed.

SOPHIE: (*Tittering a little*) Oh, my, I wasn't thinking of staying here all night.

SIMSTROM: How long *had* you planned, if it's any of my business?

SOPHIE: Just until I got the money.

SIMSTROM: Money! I thought so. Suppose you give most of it to that bellhop, Sink Lee.

SOPHIE: Oh, no, whatever money I receive goes to Madame Hegglespoon.

SIMSTROM: *Madame Hegglespoon.* That's an odd name.

SOPHIE: She'll get the money, but she won't keep it. She spends it on the girls. For food and clothing and everything.

SIMSTROM: How many . . . I mean, how many girls does she have, this Madame?

SOPHIE: Oh, there are lots. Two hundred or over. All different nationalities.

SIMSTROM: Not really!

SOPHIE: We have gay times together. (*Sophie smiles in memory for a moment, but then comes back to reality*)

SOPHIE: But I mustn't waste time like this. (*Stepping left*) About the money, Mr. Simstrom. Madame Hegglespoon said I should be brief and to the point. (*Simstrom turns over on his side and looks at Sophie for the first time*)

SOPHIE: (*After awkward pause*) Well? (*Simstrom sits up on edge of bed*)

SIMSTROM: You're not Chinese!

SOPHIE: Of course not, I'm English.

SIMSTROM: And you're so young looking. So fresh. I can't believe it. Have you been with this Madame Hegglespoon long?

SOPHIE: Oh, yes sir, since I was eight.

SIMSTROM: Eight!

SOPHIE: Well, really since I was seven and a half, but it was almost eight, so I usually say since I was eight.

SIMSTROM: You poor girl!

SOPHIE: Oh, please, Mr. Simstrom, don't feel sorry for me. They're always very kind to us, and really the girls at Madame Hegglespoon's usually have lots more fun than the girls in regular homes.

SIMSTROM: It shouldn't be permitted.

SOPHIE: Madame Hegglespoon has friends all over the city. Once a month she gives a party for outsiders to raise more money. All of the girls perform for the guests and then we play games. Madame gets lots of extra money that way.

SIMSTROM: Is your . . . house here in the city?

SOPHIE: Oh yes, our grounds are right next to the Presbyterian Mission.

SIMSTROM: How convenient.

SOPHIE: On Sundays lots of the people stop off at our place after they've been to church.

SIMSTROM: Hypocrites!

SOPHIE: I suppose it *is* wrong for people to enjoy themselves on Sunday. But I've grown to be very broad-minded while living at Madame's.

SIMSTROM: I should think so.

SOPHIE: Well, shall we talk business now?

SIMSTROM: (*Rising*) Really, my dear, I think you'd better leave.

SOPHIE: Oh, I can't, not without some money.

SIMSTROM: This woman, will she beat you?

SOPHIE: No. She's kind to all of her girls.

SIMSTROM: The police should know about her!

SOPHIE: Oh, they do. They come to all of our parties.

SIMSTROM: (*Sitting*) I've heard of Oriental corruption, but this is the worst. What about the British Embassy?

SOPHIE: Madame gets money every month from the Embassy. Not much because there aren't too many working there and most of them are married. Madame says married men don't give her as much as bachelors 'cause it takes a lot of money to support a wife these days.

SIMSTROM: (*Shaking head*) I wouldn't have believed. . . .

SOPHIE: If you give me the money, I'll hurry and leave.

SIMSTROM: You'll hurry and leave?

SOPHIE: Why yes.

SIMSTROM: Have you no ethics? You wouldn't take my money and then hurry off?

SOPHIE: Well, no, I suppose that wouldn't be very nice. I guess I could stay for a few extra moments afterwards and be sociable.

SIMSTROM: You little minx. What an actress you are! I think we'll get along beautifully together.

SOPHIE: About the money.

SIMSTROM: Well, I suppose we *must* get that out of the way first. How much?

SOPHIE: How much?

SIMSTROM: Yes, how much do you want?

SOPHIE: I don't know.

SIMSTROM: You don't know?

SOPHIE: (*Flustered*) Madame didn't say how much. She said I was to get all I could out of you.

SIMSTROM: Oh, I see. You trollops are the same the world over!

SOPHIE: (*Innocently*) How much money do you have with you?

SIMSTROM: My dear girl, didn't this Madame train you to be subtle? Or are things *usually* done this way in the Orient?

SOPHIE: (*Brightening*) Is it different in America?

SIMSTROM: (*Choking*) *Slightly*. That is . . . .

SOPHIE: About the money: Let's see. H'mm. Tell me, how much do you usually give the others?

SIMSTROM: What others?

SOPHIE: Madame Hegglespoon said others would be after you, too.

SIMSTROM: Oh God, and all I wanted was a quiet night's sleep.

SOPHIE: Then, I *am* the first one here!

SIMSTROM: Yes, you're the first, and *last,* I hope. I've just arrived in Shanghai. How could I have had relations with any others!

SOPHIE: I thought perhaps in the street. . . .

SIMSTROM: In the street! (*Rising*) How on earth can a sweet-faced girl as you. . . . It's the Orient, I guess. It hardens one to everything.

SOPHIE: (*Thinking*) Maybe you could give me a blank check and Madame could fill in the amount later.

SIMSTROM: What!

SOPHIE: It was just an idea. I'm only trying to be helpful.

SIMSTROM: Well, stop thinking so much. Girls of your profession aren't supposed to think anyway.

SOPHIE: Oh, you're wrong. Madame says we've got to learn to think for ourselves because she's raising all us girls to be wives.

SIMSTROM: Wives!

SOPHIE: Oh yes. (*Beaming*) Madame prides herself in furnishing girls who are prepared to meet whatever marriage offers.

SIMSTROM: I should presume so.

SOPHIE: About the money.

SIMSTROM: Perhaps if the Madame came up herself.

SOPHIE: (*Beginning to cry*) Oh, I've botched it! I've botched it. And I did so want to please Madame. This is the first time she's sent me out by myself and I've failed her.

SIMSTROM: This is your first time?

SOPHIE: My first time away from Madame's house. Madame would have come here herself but she said she was getting too old, and besides on Tuesdays she visits Father Regan.

SIMSTROM: A Father?

SOPHIE: He's awfully nice. Madame took me with her once, just as a kind of change, but I could see he preferred Madame to me.

SIMSTROM: She must be quite a woman.

SOPHIE: Madame is my ideal in life. I only hope that I can grow up to be like her. But I never could, I know that.

SIMSTROM: What's your name?

SOPHIE: Sophie. Sophie Higgenbottom.

SIMSTROM: Come here, Sophie. Sit down. (*Sophie sits down in the rocking chair. She finds her little jacket constricting, so she begins taking it off*)

SIMSTROM: No, leave your clothes on for awhile longer. Sophie, I want to have a talk with you. I know so little about your past because we've just met today, but I sense a tragic aura. Sophie, I feel so sorry for you.

SOPHIE: (*Beginning to cry*) You're like the rest. They all pity us girls. Oh, they pretend not to show it, but I can see. Of course, we don't live like those girls with parents, but we have gay times. Awfully gay times. We have parties. . . .

SIMSTROM: (*Pleading*) But it's wrong, Sophie, for a girl to live the way you're living. It may be all right for some other girls. But you're different. If you'd been raised in a different environment, you'd be just what you seem to be. Why, if I didn't know what I know, I'd never believe it.

SOPHIE: Please, Mr. Simstrom, don't feel upset about me. You don't have to give me the money. I don't care what Madame Hegglespoon says. There'll be other Americans.

SIMSTROM: Listen to me, Sophie. (*Crossing left. Envisioning*) There's another kind of life. One you've never even thought about, perhaps. Your life is a very unusual one. Most girls' lives are entirely different from yours. And they're happy, too. You must leave this Madame before it's too late.

SOPHIE: Leave? Why, I never want to leave! That is, until the Madame arranges it.

SIMSTROM: What do you mean?

SOPHIE: (*Brightening*) Oh, every month, men come to Madame's and take away girls. Madame arranges everything, but, of course, the girls make the decisions.

SIMSTROM: (*Muttering*) White slavery.

SOPHIE: It's so romantic. The men usually come at night and the girls go away with them with Madame at the door blessing them. Isn't it romantic?

SIMSTROM: Sophie, I've got to get you away from that place. I'm no angel, but I can see injustice. . . .

SOPHIE: But I don't want to leave. Besides, where would I go? At Madame's, the food is good, I have my own little room, and best of all, she gives each of the girls five dollars a month. And she lets us spend it any way we want.

SIMSTROM: Only five dollars!

SOPHIE: Oh, but that's really too much when a person stops to think of all we're learning from the Madame. She's training us to be professionals!

SIMSTROM: That's one word for it.

SOPHIE: I spend my five dollars a month on typing lessons.

SIMSTROM: You type?

SOPHIE: (*Nodding*) I take shorthand, too. My own system which I invented. It works fine if you dictate slowly enough. Honestly though, I can write faster in regular longhand than I can in my shorthand.

SIMSTROM: Sophie, listen carefully. (*Sitting on bed*) You're going to work for me.

SOPHIE: What!

SIMSTROM: I'm going to be here in Shanghaii for three months. I'll need a secretary. Then, when I leave, maybe I can take you with me, or else arrange for someone else to hire you.

SOPHIE: Oh, that would be wonderful! Would you pay me?

SIMSTROM: Of course.

SOPHIE: I'll give every penny to Madame. Won't that please her?

SIMSTROM: Oh, you poor innocent girl.

SOPHIE: (*Rising*) Can I leave now to go find Madame Hegglespoon? She'll be so happy.

SIMSTROM: I don't want you to see that woman ever again. Do you understand?

SOPHIE: What do you mean?

SIMSTROM: As of today, Sophie, you must change your life completely. You must never see that woman or any of those other girls again.

SOPHIE: Why, I'll see them every day. I can still live at

Madame's while I'm working for you. I'll spend my nights at the house.

SIMSTROM: No, you won't. You've got to make the break completely.

SOPHIE: But I don't want to leave. It's my home.

SIMSTROM: It isn't any longer. (*Rising*) You're too beautiful, too fine a girl to ruin your life that way. I'm going to look after you and I don't care what that Madame says.

SOPHIE: She won't be angry if you give her some money. Madame has lots of girls. They come into her every month. There are always new faces, that's why it's always so gay. At first the new girls are shy, but once we teach them things, they're awfully gay.

SIMSTROM: It's sinful. I intend to write this scandal up tonight for the papers before I go to sleep. Put on your hat, Sophie, and take me to this brothel.

SOPHIE: To what?

SIMSTROM: To the Madame's!

SOPHIE: Are you going home with me?

SIMSTROM: Yes. And I'm going to see about getting you out of that place. (*Sophie puts on her hat while Simstrom quickly puts on his shoes, tightens his tie, and puts on his coat*)

SIMSTROM: I'll fix that old monster.

SOPHIE: We'll really surprise her, won't we, Mr. Simstrom?

SIMSTROM: (*Rising*) Just call me Henry, Sophie.

SOPHIE: Oh, I can't do that.

SIMSTROM: Why not?

SOPHIE: We haven't been introduced.

SIMSTROM: Well, perhaps the Madame will introduce us properly.

SOPHIE: Of course! Then everything will be all right. You know, Mr. Simstrom, I'm so glad I came up to your room. I feel, as you say, my whole life is going to be changed.

SIMSTROM: And so will this Madame Hegglespoon's, once I lay into her.

SOPHIE: I bet she'll be awfully shocked when we walk in together. She thinks I haven't any gumption to do anything.

And wait 'til the girls see what I've brought home. (*Beaming*) They'll all be so jealous and I'll be so happy *because* they're jealous.

SIMSTROM: Come on, darling, we haven't any time to lose.

SOPHIE: Yes, let's hurry and surprise her.

SIMSTROM: We'll surprise her all right. When I meet her, I'll talk so fast and furiously, she won't be able to speak back for months. (*Quickly and loudly*) Yes sir, darling, she'll be the most surprised person in Shanghaii! (*Sophie laughs gaily and they leave hurriedly. At the door, Sophie turns around, winks, and waves happily to the audience*)

Fast Curtain

THE END

THE TRAITOR

THE TRAITOR

CHARACTERS

JIM ALLEN: A student at University College.
MIKE BADDARD: A football coach at University College

Setting: The bedroom of Jim Allen
Time: The present

THE TRAITOR

(The scene is the bedroom of Jim Allen. There is a door leading into a hallway right stage. Against the back wall, center, there is a Hollywood type bed. Against left wall there is a dresser. Some of the drawers are half open. Two chairs are downstage, one right and one left. As the scene opens we see Jim Allen putting things into a suitcase he has opened on his bed. ALLEN is a bright, intelligent looking lad in his early twenties. After a moment, there is a knock at the door. Jim closes the suitcase and puts it under bed, then crosses, opens door, and admits Mike Baddard to enter. BADDARD is a bald, flashily dressed, unintelligent looking creature in his middle forties. His manner makes us dislike him on sight. When Jim sees his visitor, he turns and walks left)

BADDARD: (*Entering*) Ain't glad to see me, are you, Allen? Well, I guess you've got reason *not* to be after what you done to me, to Brick, to University College! (*Jim is rearranging some things on his dresser, his back to Baddard*)

BADDARD: (*Looking around*) This where you live?

ALLEN: (*Half-turning*) Since you obviously got my address from the student directory, saw my name on the door downstairs, and probably were escorted here by my landlady, I'm certain that would be a *safe* assumption.

BADDARD: Now, look here, Allen. You think I'm dumb, but I ain't. I've got a *salary* which says I ain't a *bit* dumb!

ALLEN: (*Turning completely*) O.K., what's on your mind? (*Baddard grins rather greasily and sits in chair down right. He looks around for an ash tray for his cigar*)

BADDARD: Got an ash tray, kid? (*Allen shakes his head*)

BADDARD: Well, don't worry about it, kid. I can just flick the ashes here next to the wall. Your landlady must clean pretty often, I guess.

ALLEN: Flick 'em wherever you like. I want you to feel at

home. (*Baddard is too dumb to realize the barbing in this remark. Instead he feels it to be a kind welcome*)

BADDARD: That's what I can't understand about you, kid. Most of the time you're so damned pleasant and cooperative, but after this thing you done to us last night, I can't make you out at all.

ALLEN: That shouldn't give you any trouble, Coach Baddard. I'm just an ordinary run-of-the mill guy. And probably not too bright.

BADDARD: Talk sense, willya! Has Brick been by?

ALLEN: No.

BADDARD: I suppose you heard what happened?

ALLEN: About the test?

BADDARD: Yeah.

ALLEN: (*Sincerely*) Too bad.

BADDARD: Too bad! Jeez, kid, a catastrophe! Our best football player flunking his Biology mid-term.

ALLEN: It's been flunked before. By others.

BADDARD: Who in Hell cares about . . . others. Brick, our Brick Bradford flunked it. Flunking mid-terms keeps men off the football field. You knew that, didn't ya, kid?

ALLEN: It's a campus rumor.

BADDARD: (*Rising*) Whyja do it, kid? Whyja do it to Brick . . . and to me.

ALLEN: I'd rather not talk about it. Let's forget the whole thing. (*Baddard walks quickly over to Allen and grabs him by the back of his collar*)

BADDARD: We *ain't* forgettin' it, Allen. People don't treat Mike Baddard the way you did last night and get off easy. (*Allen breaks loose, walks toward door, and opens it*)

ALLEN (*Quietly*) You can leave now, Coach Baddard. (*Baddard looks at Allen for a moment, then shrugs, smiles a bit, and sits in chair left*)

BADDARD: We've always been friends, Allen. What happened? Where was you last night?

ALLEN: I was out.

BADDARD: (*Quickly*) Out where!

ALLEN: Walking.

BADDARD: Jeez, you was out walking and Brick bleeding to death without you.

ALLEN: I'd forgotten all about *him.*

BADDARD: Forgotten Brick! How couldja? How couldja forget last night about Brick's Biology mid-term today. How couldja?

ALLEN: I had other things on my mind.

BADDARD: What kind of guy are you, anyway? Don't you know what Brick means to me, to this school, your old school. Where in the Hell's your spirit, your honor? Do you want to see University College disgraced down on that football field? On the great field of glory? Do you want to see your old almer mater go under? (*Allen closes the door silently and then sits in chair right*)

BADDARD: Before, you've always been so cooperative, kid. Our Brick ain't dumb, nobody says that, but he just ain't got enough time to study for these classes. That's why I count on loyal ones like you assisting your old school by helping Brick stay on the team.

ALLEN: Yes, I guess that's mighty important.

BADDARD: And you've done a wonderful job, kid. Up to last night. What went wrong? In all those other classes, you seemed to know just what the profs would ask and you helped Brick beautifully. But now, today—this Biology mid-term—flunked cold!

ALLEN: I called Brick up night before last and offered to help him.

BADDARD: He had to be somewhere else that night.

ALLEN: Yeah, I hear she's a nice lay.

BADDARD: Now, kid, that ain't a sportin' thing to say. But let's forget it. That ain't important. What you did last night *is.* Brick came here last night at eight with his books. He stayed here until eleven o'clock waiting for you, then went home to bed.

ALLEN: I heard the mid-term was easy. Brick should've remembered enough from the lectures to have passed it.

BADDARD: (*Rising*) Ya keep forgetting, kid, Brick ain't

ordinary. He can't be expected to sit there and understand what that Biology prof is saying when his head is full-up of the plays and things I've drilled into him. You gotta put first things first.

ALLEN: I guess you're right. The Biology prof makes $3,000 a year and you make, what is it now, 15 or 16,000? I guess that makes you more worth listening to.

BADDARD: $3,000 is too much for that . . . the trouble he gave me. But he reconsidered. He went back over Brick's test and found a few things were better than when he first read them.

ALLEN: You saw the alumni head who saw the president who saw the Biology prof who suddenly decided that Brick's paper was good enough to pass the mid-term. Very nice. Your worries are over, Coach Baddard. Brick will play and our honor will go unsullied.

BADDARD: (*Crossing right*) You think you're pretty smart, don't you?

ALLEN: (*Rises, crosses left*) At this moment, I feel like I've been the dumbest guy on earth here at University College. (*Allen reaches down, picks up suitcase, and throws it on bed*)

ALLEN: For three years I've been working in pre-med, just waiting for the day when I could enter medical school. Hit that last lap, then go out and help the world with my knowledge of medicine. It was a pretty idealistic dream.

BADDARD: What the Hell do I care about your dream?

ALLEN: That's it, you don't. I met Brick when we were freshmen. He'd received a scholarship. The alumni paid the rent on his apartment and he got all his meals free from the University. I didn't see him very often because I worked thirty hours a week and took my courses in anatomy, chemistry, physics, and all the rest.

BADDARD: I don't see what this has got to do. . . .

ALLEN: (*Interrupting*) I didn't have time to play college boy along with the others, scream at the rallies, and worship the football players. I had a dream. A dream I knew would come true if I just held to my course. I helped Brick a little that first year because I felt sorry for him. Next year I had to work more hours because rents went up and food was higher. My courses were stiffer but I made out. Then you came to me.

BADDARD: (*Sitting in chair right*) Because I knew you to be a good, red-blooded American boy.

ALLEN: (*Stepping out*) How little you know. You asked me, pleaded with me, to help Brick just once more. Well, that once more turned into helping him before every exam. Drilling into him the answers to the questions I thought the profs would ask.

BADDARD: Brick liked you. And he will again when he forgets about last night.

ALLEN: Look, Coach, you can take Brick and all the rest like him and flush 'em down the nearest toilet.

BADDARD: Now kid, you ain't talkin' like a real American.

ALLEN: At the moment I don't feel like that's a very high ambition.

BADDARD: You sure talk crazy sometimes. Let's forget I came. Brick'll be in to see you tomorrow. I'll tell him to patch things up 'cause you're the only one who can get him through the final exam.

ALLEN: I won't be here tomorrow. (*Baddard starts to speak, but Allen continues*) I had a pretty good grade average in spite of everything. But it's been going down. Brick's been doing less and less work, so it's taken more and more time for cramming. Well, a week ago I stayed up all night working with Brick. He was tired from being out four nights in a row, but he had a bad exam the next day. I had a mid-term myself but I thought I could pass it O.K. and spent all my time helping Brick. Well, yesterday, I got the result. I flunked that mid-term.

BADDARD: (*Amazed*) You, kid?

ALLEN: I have to have a B plus average to get into medical school. I can't get it now with this flunk, so med school is out. Everything is over.

BADDARD: And you're leaving University College?

ALLEN: Yes, leaving.

BADDARD: But where to?

ALLEN: I don't know yet. Far, far away. To some place

where there's a sense of values that's worthwhile. Some place where football coaches don't make more than college presidents. Some place, . . . oh . . . what's the use.

BADDARD: Look, kid, reconsider. (*Rising*) You're turning . . . *traitor*. You can't do this to Brick. (*Allen crosses to bureau left, takes out travelling kit, returns and places it in suitcase*)

ALLEN: Brick isn't worth saving. When you're through with him, you'll kick him out with the *rest* of the *junk* you scrap every year.

BADDARD: (*Pointing*) Look, kid, I'm too big a man to take this kind of guff from you. I can screw you for life with *all* the universities.

ALLEN: I'm behind schedule in packing, so will you please leave. (*Slowly, quietly, but with great intensity*) You low, crawling, . . . son of a bitch. (*Baddard looks at Jim in a dazed, shocked way, then turns and leaves in a huff. Jim looks after him for a moment, then continues with his packing as the curtains slowly close*)

THE END

RAIN ON THE OCEAN

RAIN ON THE OCEAN

CHARACTERS

JIM HILL, a farmer
MARY HILL, his wife

Setting: A Southwestern farm
Time: The present

RAIN ON THE OCEAN

(The setting is the living room of Jim and Mary Hill in a drab, sun-scorched section of the Southwest. The play opens on Jim Hill who is sitting at a table, head in arms. JIM is in his early thirties, a tired, haggard, disillusioned man. After the curtains part, he opens a Bible and begins reading softly.)

JIM: (*Reading*) His children are far from safety, and they are crushed in the gate, neither is there any to deliver them. Whose harvest the hungry eateth up, and taketh it even out of the thorns, and the robber swalloweth up their substance. Although affliction cometh not forth of the dust, neither doth trouble spring out of the ground. Yet man is born unto trouble, as the sparks fly upward. I would seek unto God, and unto God would I commit my cause. (*Jim looks up, clenches his fists in front of him, and begins muttering a prayer*)

JIM: (*Pleading*) God, can't you hear any of our prayers? Just a little rain, please, not to save our crops, but our soil. Everything's burned to blackness, and now the soil is all loose and ready to blow away. Dear God, if *I've* sinned, punish *me*, but don't punish my family. Mary. The children. Oh God, what have I done? (*Mary Hill enters from left. MARY is about the same age as her husband and possesses, like him, a tired gauntness. She looks at her husband on entering but says nothing. Instead, she circles slowly behind the table, then sits on a rocker downstage right and begins to rock slowly, looking out in front of her*)

MARY: Pattie cried out in her sleep. Jimmy is still awake. His little stomach won't let him sleep—it keeps crying out for food which will stick to his bones, Solid, proper food.

JIM: (*Hopelessly*) We're all through here.

MARY: (*Sadly*) And it was going to be so wonderful.

JIM: (*Looking out*) Our own farm, worked and tilled with our own hands, providing us with life.

MARY: (*Matter-of-factly*) Life.

JIM: Why must living be so hard? Sometimes it seems God doesn't *want* us to live.

MARY: The flowers live easily. The birds. But Nature is enemy to man. And if Nature be God. . . .

JIM: (*Musingly*) Then God is our enemy. (*Mary begins to say something but doesn't. She looks out in a shock of realization*)

JIM: (*Thoughtfully*) We are constantly at battle with Nature. Weeds grow where we plant seeds. When we need rain, there is none, and when we need sunshine in deep winter, there is nothing but freezing blizzard upon blizzard. Look about the earth, Mary. What is good is man-made. In order to live we must create our own shelters, grow our own food. Fighting disease, decay, death. The forces of Nature seem designed only to defeat Man. (*Bitterly*) To force him again to his animal state where his only role is to breed . . . and breed . . . endlessly.

MARY: (*Quickly*) These are wicked thoughts, Jim.

JIM: We were foolish to pray. (*Rising*) Pray to what! A God who sends persecution after persecution. We've been poor in spirit, that's where we've been wrong. We've submitted with prayers instead of fighting back. Why is it always the religious ones who have the most trouble? I think it's because God has contempt for our weakness.

MARY: (*Slowly*) I brought down the three suitcases from the attic.

JIM: Will they be enough?

MARY: Yes.

JIM: When shall we leave?

MARY: In the morning. Early, before the sun becomes too blazing. Once we get to the highway perhaps a truck will pick us up. (*Jim sits again in chair at table*)

JIM: The end. . . .

MARY: Maybe if we go in twos, we'll get along easier. I could take Pattie, and you, Jimmy. Four's a lot for anyone to stop for.

JIM: Where do you want to go?

MARY: It doesn't matter.

JIM: The city? (*Mary flinches slightly at the word*)

JIM: They say there's no work there, but I'll find something. I've a little strength left, and a back someone might wish to hire.

MARY: The city is so terrifying. Even worse than here. Here we have a roof.

JIM: But no food.

MARY: People in cities are cold and unfriendly. Especially to those with no money who have children. They'll say we're tramps. Perhaps the police will pick us up and. . . .

JIM: Don't worry now.

MARY: We worked so hard here on the farm. (*Rises from rocker*) Always up before sunrise and never getting to bed until our tired bodies were about to collapse. All these years . . . and nothing to show for it.

JIM: If we still had our car, we could sleep in it. (*Mary circles right behind rocker and places her hands on its back*)

MARY: Everyone in the city pays rent and food comes from restaurants and stores. That means money. Lots of it.

JIM: I'll find something to do.

MARY: If God hates us so much, why doesn't He kill us all off at once?

JIM: Then the game would be over. (*Bitterly*) It's more fun for Him this way. A hurricane here, a tornado over there, earthquakes, floods, and always a war *somewhere* on the globe.

MARY: People cause wars, not God.

JIM: God put warfare into people's hearts. It's the same thing. (*Mary crosses over to behind Jim and puts her left hand on his left shoulder*)

MARY: We were wrong to have children. Living isn't worth the trouble.

JIM: People have children because they're selfish—children who are born naked into the world. Animals are clothed naturally, but not humans. Only humans have to provide, struggle for clothing, housing, food. (*Sadly*) We're not meant for this world. We're aliens, all of us. (*Bitterly*) Existing only for the cat and mouse game God's always playing up there.

MARY: We'd better try and get some sleep, Jim, if we're to start early. (*Mary begins to walk left*)

JIM: The sun's still out.

MARY: It's after eight though. (*Mary continues walking toward doorway left. As she does so her attention is caught by something she sees out the window. She stops, looks at Jim, then goes rather quickly to the window*)

MARY: Jim!

JIM: What's the matter?

MARY: Come to the window. (*Jim gets up and goes over to the window*)

MARY: That blackness in the East.

JIM: (*Softly*) An Eastern rain.

MARY: An Eastern rain at last.

JIM: It's coming closer.

MARY: And so large. Larger all the time.

JIM: After all these months. Thank God!

MARY: Yes, thank God. (*Turning to Jim*) Oh Jim, how could we have said those things we did. God was testing us and we failed Him.

JIM: We've no crops to take the water.

MARY: No. But we've the loose dry soil thirsting for rain. Now we can plant. Oh, we'll make out somehow. As long as we've moist soil. (*They walk together toward table*)

JIM: Should we awaken the children?

MARY: No, let them sleep. Oh, Jim, we won't have to go to the city now. The terrible city. (*Mary cries softly, leaning against Jim. Jim takes her into his arms*)

MARY: After our crop's in again, and things growing, maybe we can paint the house, and get some new curtains, red gingham ones for our kitchen. Oh, it'll be wonderful, Jim. Here in our own little world. We'll have so much food. I'll can every bit. We'll never have that thin soup again! (*Mary begins to laugh, and Jim joins her. Mary then begins rubbing her eye. She takes up her apron and tries to get an irritant out of her eye, not thinking much of it*)

JIM: (*Releasing Mary*) Something in your eye?

MARY: It's nothing.

JIM: Here, take my handkerchief. (*Jim and Mary are still in high spirits as Mary takes the foreign object out of her eye*)

MARY: (*Smiling*) There! I guess it was just a speck of dust. (*After she's said the word, she stops a moment, as if horror-strickened. A moment later, Jim goes to the window left*)

MARY: (*Crossing right fearfully*) Rain *always* comes from the East this time of year. Hear the wind, Jim, an Eastern wind bringing rain.

JIM: (*Quietly*) There's a wind all right.

MARY: And the rain cloud. The huge, black rain cloud. (*Jim comes back to the table and sits down slowly*)

JIM: Only dust. (*Jim and Mary are both frozen for a moment. The wind knocks open a window to the left of them. Both look and watch the dust beginning to blow in. Then Jim places his head on his arms and begins to sob softly. Mary goes over to Jim, places her right hand on his right shoulder, her back to the audience, and looks over at the opened window as the curtains slowly close*)

THE END

WAITING

WAITING

CHARACTERS

MADAME, an older woman
FRANÇOIS, an older girl
FRANCIS, a boy

Setting: Pigalle, Paris
Time: The present or the past

WAITING

(The setting is steps in front of a black curtain which is closed but parted slightly in the middle. When lights are raised there is revealed François, who is painted and dressed as a young girl. She sits on steps looking blankly in front of her. After a moment Madame Blau approaches with Francis. Madame Blau is a buxom, hard-faced woman in her fifties. Francis is a youth in his teens).

MADAME: (*To François*) This is Francis. (*François looks up at him without display of great interest and motions for him to sit beside her, which he does. Madame Blau leaves. Francis looks at her for a moment and then looks out blankly also. After a moment he turns to François and speaks softly to her*)

FRANCIS: What's your name? (*François looks at Francis for a moment, then looks out again*)

FRANÇOIS: (*Matter-of-factly*) Does it matter? (*Francis looks at her and then looks out again. Both look out. Then François speaks without looking at Francis*)

FRANÇOIS: Do you like . . . *François?* (*Francis doesn't look at François*)

FRANCIS: Very much.

FRANÇOIS: Then call me that. (*Both continue to look out*)

FRANCIS: The regular boy is sick.

FRANÇOIS: Hah! That's his story!

FRANCIS: (*Turning to François, attempting to control his eagerness*) You mean he might not be back?

FRANÇOIS: He'll be back when he's been thrown out . . . (*Looking at Francis*) You're a lot younger.

FRANCIS: I'm seventeen.

FRANÇOIS: I'm not! (*Another long pause*) We follow the the dog act. (*Francis looks at François and she motions toward curtain. Francis rises slowly and looks through curtain*)

FRANÇOIS: We are called "Young Love." (*Francis turns

away from the curtain and slowly returns and sits near François —closer this time)

FRANCIS (*Softly*) I need the money. I hope I'm good enough. . . . It's so strange . . . the quietness of the audience I mean . . . I thought there'd be more noise.

FRANÇOIS: No noise. Each watcher is a performer himself. Each plays the performer's role.

FRANCIS: I hope I am satisfactory.

FRANÇOIS: You are young. That is for contrast.

FRANCIS: I see.

FRANÇOIS: Bordeaux?

FRANCIS: No, Rouen.

FRANÇOIS: Student?

FRANCIS: For awhile.

FRANÇOIS: And now?

FRANCIS: (*After a pause*) This. (*After a pause*) I need this job . . . Could you help me. (*François looks at Francis for a moment*)

FRANÇOIS: Why did you leave Rouen?

FRANCIS: I wanted to be where life is.

FRANÇOIS: (*Motioning to curtains*) There is life . . . (*Turning to Francis*) Are you a poet?

FRANCIS: I once thought so . . . Words should make the spirit soar, but my words do not.

FRANÇOIS: Why did you come here?

FRANCIS: I have no money. (*Simply*) I am hungry. (*There is another pause. Both look out*)

FRANÇOIS: (*Simply*) I hate men.

FRANCIS: (*Simply*) I'm sorry.

FRANÇOIS: I could get another job if I wanted.

FRANCIS: Will you help me?

FRANÇOIS: Why should I?

FRANCIS: Because I need your help.

FRANÇOIS: The other boy, when he returns, will need work also.

FRANCIS: Please help me.

FRANÇOIS: I once went to Rouen. It is a quiet town and

there are green fields all around. And Joan of Arc was burned there.

FRANCIS: Yes, Joan of Arc was burned there.

FRANÇOIS: It must be awful to be burned. To be alive and to be burned.

FRANCIS: Please help me. (*There is a pause*)

FRANÇOIS: (*Slowly*) You must fumble as a young boy. That is your part. You must undress me, but not look at me. Then, you must disrobe, turning your back to me. Then . . . then . . . as you make love . . . you must look only into my eyes, and you must be awkward, but gentle, and look only into my eyes. (*François looks ahead still. Francis places his hands tenderly on hers as Madame Blau approaches and nods toward curtain. Both rise and step through curtain as lights on stage dim out*)

END

THE CONTESSA

THE CONTESSA

CHARACTERS

THE CONTESSA
MARCELLO, her son
CONCETTA, her maid
MRS. GASBY, an American from New Jersey

Setting: Rome. A room in home of The Contessa
Time: The present

THE CONTESSA

(The Contessa is sitting in a satin chair as her grandson is looking out the window. The Contessa is in her sixties. Her grandson is in his early twenties. After the curtains have parted, Marcello looks away from the window).

MARCELLO: Her car has arrived.

CONTESSA: A vulgar Cadillac, no doubt.

MARCELLO: No, an English Ford, I believe.

CONTESSA: Oh, Marcello, my child, how your grandmama has slipped in this world. (*Marcello crosses over and kisses the Contessa*)

CONTESSA: What have I to look forward to? Nothing. All that is left to me in this life is a whoring grandson. (*Sighing*) Ring for Concetta, please. (*Marcello walks right and pulls a cord*)

MARCELLO: I'll go down and meet the lady. (*As Marcello exits right, Concetta the maid enters from left*)

CONCETTA: You rang, Contessa?

CONTESSA: The American has arrived. Please bring the tea things as quickly as possible. I do not wish our encounter to be any longer than necessary. (*Concetta begins to leave*)

CONTESSA: Oh, Concetta. (*Concetta turns*) Please bring me my fan off the desk. (*Concetta does so and then leaves left. The Contessa arranges herself in a regal position. Marcello enters with Mrs. Gasby, a smartly-dressed American in her forties*)

MARCELLO: Grandmama, this is Mrs. Harry Gasby, from America. (*The Contessa nods*)

MRS. GASBY: (*Stepping forward*) How do you do, Contessa. It was so good of you to receive me.

CONTESSA: (*Regally*) Do sit down. I've already ordered tea.

MRS. GASBY: That's wonderful as I really don't have much time.

CONTESSA: Oh? (*This comes as a surprise to the Contessa. She begins using her fan and does so occasionally throughout rest of play*)

MRS. GASBY: I suppose being in a rush is one of the American characteristics.

CONTESSA: Yes, unfortunately.

MRS. GASBY: But then, we do get things done, don't we, Contessa?

CONTESSA: I'm afraid I have had little experience with things American.

MRS. GASBY: What a pity! (*Concetta enters with tea things and places them on the table in front of the Contessa. The Contessa begins pouring tea into a cup*)

CONTESSA: Cream or lemon?

MRS. GASBY: (*Sweetly*) Neither. (*The Contessa hands the cup to Concetta, who takes it to Mrs. Gasby. The Contessa nods to Concetta to leave and she does. Mrs. Gasby takes one sip of tea, puts it down and does not pick up the cup again*)

MARCELLO: Mrs. Gasby's husband is in plumbing. New Jersey, I believe.

MRS. GASBY: East Rutherford, to be exact. Harry is most interested in the common market.

CONTESSA: (*Rather chillily*) Interest in things common seems to be the blight of our era.

MARCELLO: Mrs. Gasby's husband is planning to open a branch office here in Rome.

CONTESSA: Then you'll be living here, be part of our little social world.

MRS. GASBY: Only for awhile. Harry and I prefer London and, of course, Paris. We'll be here only as long as necessary.

CONTESSA: But even so you'll want to be properly presented.

MRS. GASBY: Yes, that is why Mrs. Bloomsdale arranged for us to meet.

CONTESSA: Mrs. Bloomsdale and I have been friends since the first World War. The Americans have changed I've noticed.

MRS. GASBY: The world does move on.

CONTESSA: A proper introduction to Rome Society is most important.

MRS. GASBY: Oh, indeed.

CONTESSA: One's existence and happiness in Rome depend on it.

MRS. GASBY: You are so right, Contessa.

MARCELLO: Unfortunately, Grandmama, Mrs. Gasby must leave Rome . . . temporarily . . . at the end of the month.

MRS. GASBY: Yes, on September 29.

CONTESSA: Oh, how unfortunate!

MRS. GASBY: Why, dear lady?

CONTESSA: I am at the utter control of my banker and will not have my next quarter's allowance until October 1. I would not dream of presenting you to Rome society unless it could be done properly.

MRS. GASBY: Oh, but you must allow me to help.

CONTESSA: Don't speak of it, dear lady.

MRS. GASBY: I insist! A quiet affair with, say, about a hundred of your friends, with a minimum of ten titles.

CONTESSA: Ten titles?

MRS. GASBY: Perhaps a garden party. A gala with costumes. In your garden. Music and lanterns. (*Goes to window*) Oh dear, the garden needs a great deal of work, doesn't it? Pity! Well, perhaps a ball. (*Looking around*) This room needs redecorating. If we had a ball with just candlelight, perhaps it wouldn't show. Let's see, a ball, for one hundred people, with minimum of ten titles. Dinner, champagne, the orchestra, attendants. (*Sitting again*) How much would that amount to, Contessa?

CONTESSA: (*Thinking quickly*) There are always extras, so it is difficult to be exact.

MRS. GASBY: Approximately, Contessa.

CONTESSA: As you say, much work must be done. I think perhaps about 15,000 lire.

MRS. GASBY: That's $2400.00.

CONTESSA: More or less.

MRS. GASBY: And you'll guarantee ten titles.

CONTESSA: Yes.

MRS. GASBY: I think the Saturday before I leave would be most appropriate.

CONTESSA: (*To Marcello*) Bring me my appointment book, will you, Marcello? (*Marcello crosses left to desk and returns with book and hands it to Contessa who flips through pages. Marcello stands behind Contessa*)

CONTESSA: Yes, that will be most satisfactory.

MRS. GASBY: And will your grandson be free that evening? I have a daughter about his age who will be needing an escort.

MARCELLO: I shall be most delighted, Mrs. Gasby.

MRS. GASBY: She has a beau back home—a sophomore at Princeton. We're quite pleased with him, but he won't be able to fly over. So its' *just an escort* we're interested in. Are you titled.

MARCELLO: Yes, Mrs. Gasby, I am titled.

MRS. GASBY: That will look well in the papers.

CONTESSA: The papers. I forgot. And the photographers. That will be extra. About 1,000 lire.

MRS. GASBY: Another $160.00.

CONTESSA: It will be best for me to make the contacts. Actually, some of them are friends of Marcello.

MRS. GASBY: *Indeed?* I've always considered newsmen and their photographers a rather low lot. (*Looking around*) It'd be a pity to change anything here. There's such a charming decadence about it all. The smaller salon I passed through is rather smart.

CONTESA: (*Stiffly*) That is the only room we've done over.

MRS. GASBY: One could entertain there, couldn't one?

CONTESSA: Why, I suppose one could.

MRS. GASBY: For tea, perhaps.

CONTESSA: I suppose for only tea.

MRS. GASBY: How much, Contessa, for afternoon tea with ten titles and your grandson to escort my daughter, and newsmen and photographers.

CONTESSA: Instead of the ball?

MRS. GASBY: Instead of the ball.

CONTESSA: About 6,000 lire.

MRS. GASBY: That's about $960.00. (*Rising*) I'm afraid that is a little steep. The Princess Ragsveil will give me a tea with twelve titles, newsmen and photographers for $800.00.

CONTESSA: Princess Ragsveil!

MRS. GASBY: (*Bitchily*) I'm such a dumbell about titles, but isn't a princess higher than a contessa?

CONTESSA: It is the family that matters. (*Mrs. Gasby takes out checkbook and sits in chair*)

MRS. GASBY: Shall we say 700 American dollars. Half now and half upon appearance of the ten titles, newsmen and photographers. (*Contessa looks angrily at Marcello who hesitates a moment and then nods to Contessa*)

CONTESSA: I like the directness you Americans display. Most of the Americans I've known were of the older breed. Innocents who displayed some awe of position and the old titled families.

MRS. GASBY: Time does move on, doesn't it, Contessa?

CONTESSA: Yes, fortunately. I am wondering, Mrs. Gasby, if you could possibly make out the check for the full amount.

MRS. GASBY: $700.00?

CONTESSA: Yes, if it wouldn't be inconvenient.

MRS. GASBY: My husband wouldn't, but I feel I can trust you.

CONTESSA: We are an old family. Our word is as treasure. (*Mrs. Gasby writes out the check, rises and hands it to Contessa who takes it*)

CONTESSA: I'll have *this* room done over, made presentable. And I'll invite the ten titles and others, old friends of good families, and my grandson will escort your daughter, and there will be newsmen and photographers and you will be properly introduced into Rome society. It will be a gracious introduction, with dignity. (*Rising*) And it will be my gift to you, Mrs. Gasby. (*Contessa begins tearing the check into shreds and letting them drop to the floor*)

CONTESSA: Until we meet again, Mrs. Gasby, at your tea. (*Mrs. Gasby is bewildered*)

CONTESSA: Marcello, please escort Mrs. Gasby to the door. (*Marcello steps right*)

CONTESSA: Goodbye, Mrs. Gasby, until the tea.

MRS. GASBY: There's surely a mistake . . .

CONTESSA: (*Proudly*) A mistake? Whose, Mrs. Gasby? Whose? (*The Contessa smiles victoriously as Marcello escorts Mrs. Gasby out of the room*)

END

OCCASION

OCCASION

CHARACTER

Miss Andrews

Setting: Her apartment
Time: The present

OCCASION

(Miss Mary Andrews, a private secretary in her early forties, enters a tight living room of a second class residential hotel. She is carrying groceries, etc., which she takes into her small kitchenette. A moment later she returns to the living room and begins taking off her hat and coat. These she places on a chair. Then Miss Andrews sits down, kicks off shoes, and lies back relaxed. A moment later Miss Andrews looks around slowly. She then gets up, walks around the room and touches various items. She then goes over to the wall, takes the earphone of her apartment intercommunication unit, and places it to her ear. Mary pushes the buzzer of the unit and soon speaks into the mouthpiece).

MISS ANDREWS: Hello, Mr. Garson? This is Miss Andrews in apartment 416. I was wondering, if by chance, there was a letter for me that you might have overlooked in delivering today. (*Pause*) No letter? I see. Were there any callers? I mean anyone who called but didn't leave names? None? None at all. Thank you, Mr. Garson. (*As after-thought*) It was nice talking to you. (*Miss Andrews puts the earpiece back slowly on the hook, looks about her, then goes slowly into the kitchenette, and brings out a birthday cake which she places on the table center stage. She then lights the candles and sits at left side of table watching the burning candles. After a moment she begins singing softly*)

MISS ANDREWS: (*Singing*) Happy Birthday to Me,
Happy Birthday to Me,
Happy Birthday, Dear Mary,
Happy Birthday to Me.

(*Miss Andrews look at the cake for a moment more, then buries her head in arms and begins to cry as curtains close*)

THE END

REMEMBRANCE

REMEMBRANCE

CHARACTERS

PAUL CAILLOT, a bachelor in his thirties
MME. RAMIEUX, a married woman in her forties

Setting: Caillot's studio in Paris
Time: The past

REMEMBRANCE

(The scene is the studio of Paul Caillot. When the scene opens Caillot is playing at his harpsicord, making notations on the musical score frequently as he plays and composes. After a moment there is a knock at the door right. Caillot continues playing. Again there is the knocking).

CAILLOT: Entrez. (*Mme. Raimeux enters—a beautiful woman in her forties. When Paul sees her, he motions her to a chair. Mme Raimeux is indignant, but seats herself. After a moment Paul stops his playing but does not look at Mme Raimeux*)

MME RAIMEUX: (*Indignantly*) Monsieur Caillot, I came only to tell you in person what an arrogant, detestable person I think you are. (*Paul does not look at her but makes a notation with pencil on his score*)

MME RAMIEUX: (*Continuing*) I am not like the other women in Paris, available at your slightest bidding. The idea! A formal reception. Our first meeting. And I, the wife of France's leading industrialist. Such affrontry! To invite me here at this hour. A formal reception. Our first meeting. I, a married woman. A woman of honor and respect. A woman whose reputation is untarnished. Oh, I've heard of your successes! All Paris has. Even the details are known! Oh, the affrontry! The insult! I have come only to let you know there is one woman in France who is impervious to your seemingly insatiable desires. (*Paul still doesn't look at her, but makes a notation with pencil on his score*)

MME RAMIEUX: (*Rising*) I am leaving. Still a woman of respect. (*Goes to door, but turns*) Have you nothing to say?

CAILLOT: (*Indicating*) The screen is over there. (*Mme Raimeux pauses at the door*)

MME RAMIEUX: (*Softly, with horror*) It's true. Every word. A beast. Only a beast.

CAILOT: (*Softly*) True. Every word. True.

MME RAMIEUX: A formal reception. Our first meeting. Your impossible invitation.

CAILLOT. You are here.

MME RAMIEUX: Only to let you know the impossibility of your proposal.

CAILLOT: (*After pause*) Leave, if you like.

MME RAMIEUX: Why would I stay.

CAILLOT: No reason, really.

MME RAMIEUX: No reason.

CAILLOT: My invitation to you had one intent only.

MME RAMIEUX: Beast!

CAILLOT: You are the wife of our country's leading industrialist. That is true. A woman of honor and respect. A woman whose reputation is untarnished. All true. True. That is how all Paris views you. But not how I view you. (*Mme Ramieux holds her breath slightly*) I view you only as a desirable woman to lure into my bed.

MME RAMIEUX: At a formal reception. Our first meeting. I have a soul. You might have been interested in that.

CAILLOT: Your soul does not interest me.

MME RAMIEUX: You have probably never before met a woman of such great respectability.

CAILLOT: That is true.

MME RAMIEUX: And your only desire is to bring about my ruin.

CAILLOT: My only desire is to bed you.

MME RAMIEUX: You are mad.

CAILLOT: Leave if you like.

MME RAMIEUX: All Paris knows of your reputation.

CAILLOT: That I can have anyone I want . . . (*Turning directly to her*) You are ten years older than I . . . Even your husband would be proud to hear I desired you.

MME RAMIEUX: He knows. (*Stepping left*) All Paris knows. (*Caillot turns away and begins playing softly again*)

MME RAMIEUX: Men hired by my husband followed me here. If I should remain a moment longer it will be all over

Paris that I have become your lover. That a woman ten years older has become your mistress. (*Caillot continues his playing*)

MME RAMIEUX: (*Plaintively*) Do you truly desire me?

CAILLOT: (*Simply*) I am a man.

MME RAMIEUX: My soul, truly I have a beautiful soul . . . (*Caillot waves a hand toward her in annoyance*)

MME RAMIEUX: (*Turning right and speaking almost to herself*) I am lost. (*Caillot stops his playing*)

CAILLOT: In forty years you will be eighty. I shall be dead. Composers die young. And when you are eighty, what will you have to tell—to think about? What will they whisper about behind your back when you are eighty years old? One thing. That when you were forty you were seduced—by Paul Caillot, the composer who was thirty years old and had his pick of Paris . . . (*Spoken softly, after a pause*) Go, my dear, if you must.

MME RAMIEUX: (*Very softly*) You would not send me away.

CAILLOT: I am a cruel man. Brutal. A beast.

MME RAMIEUX: (*Softly*) You would not send me away. (*Caillot softly folds his hands in his lap and looks directly at Mme Ramieux*)

CALLOT: What will you tell people when you are eighty.

MME RAMIEUX: (*Turning to him hypnotically*) That I was seduced by a man ten years younger. A man who had no interest in my soul. A man consumed in desire . . . Desire for me.

CAILLOT: (*Softly, pathetically*) I am a cruel man. A brutal man.

MME RAMIEUX: (*With great feeling*) You are Paul Caillot! (*They look at each other for a moment, then Mme Ramieux goes toward the screen as Paul Caillot commences his playing again and the curtains close*)

END

SCENE

SCENE

CHARACTERS

FRANK
KENNY
BERNADETTE

Setting: A room in a bachelor apartment
Time: The present

SCENE

(As the scene opens, Kenny, a young man in his mid-twenties, stands in front of a mirror putting on his tie. He addresses his remarks to someone in adjoining room).

KENNY: Still wish you'd change your mind and go with us, Frank. Just think, one poor little ole extra girl with no one but Kenny Boy to take care of her.

FRANK: (*Offstage voice*) Only *one* extra should prove no problem for you, Kenny. (*Frank, a man in his late twenties, enters in his stocking feet and carries a tie. He walks over to behind Kenny and looks over Kenny's shoulder into the mirror as he fixes his tie*) I'm meeting Bernadette at nine. To go look at drapery materials.

KENNY: Real lively evening. How's the house coming?

FRANK: Fine.

KENNY: And your trip. Still Bermuda?

FRANK: Yeah, that's not much of a honeymoon. Two weeks in Bermuda, but the house is costing us a lot more than we'd planned. (*Frank goes over to sofa chair right, sits, and begins putting on his shoes which are nearby*)

KENNY: You're both very lucky people. You and this Bernadette. (*Brushing his hair*) That's what we all want. A nice decent girl. To love, and to marry, and to settle down.

FRANK: Can't see you ever settling down.

KENNY: If I could meet just one nice girl.

FRANK: There're lots of nice girls, Kenny. All around. Just be nice yourself and you'll meet them.

KENNY: Just be nice, he says. I try to, Frank, but happens? I go into action. Knock 'em off. Don't mean to, don't even try half the time. Just reflex action. (*Frank laughs*)

KENNY: And I hate myself afterwards. Cause it was all so easy. And cause it means nothing to me. Nothing at all.

FRANK: I pity you, Kenny, I really do.

KENNY: Go on, it's not that bad.

FRANK: Being so compulsive about sex. Lining 'em up and knockin' 'em down. Just like an animal. Where's the fun?

KENNY: No fun at all. (*Frank rises, puts on coat, and goes to door*)

FRANK: Well, best of luck tonight, Kenny, with both of them. But you're the last guy I know who needs the luck! (*Frank laughs and leaves. Kenny goes into bedroom area and returns with coat which he puts on. He then again looks into mirror and brushes his hair. The telephone rings*)

KENNY: Hello . . . What? Well, why can't she come to the phone herself? Where are you? Let me talk to Nancy; I'm pretty damned uphappy about this . . . Hello . . . Hello . . . (*Kenny in disbelief hangs up phone, then becomes a little angry. He goes to mirror and with his hand, messes up his hair. The doorbell of the apartment rings. He is surprised, but hopeful. He attempts to smooth his hair with his hands as he crosses right to doorway. He soon reappears with Bernadette. Bernadette is an Italian type, clean-cut girl in her early twenties*)

KENNY: So you're Frank's girl.

BERNADETTE: Fiancée.

KENNY: Well, I can understand now why he never brought you around!

BERNADETTE: I got off work a little early and just took a chance Frank might still be here. I won't bother you, Mr. . . . (*Bernadette turns to leave*)

KENNY: The name is Kenny. But don't rush off. Stay for one drink.

BERNADETTE: I really mustn't.

KENNY: That's not being very hospitable. Here I am, Frank's roommate, his best friend, and you won't even stay for one drink to toast my pal's forthcoming marriage.

BERNADETTE: (*Smiling*) You've shamed me into it. (*Sitting on sofa*) But only one. (*Kenny goes over to bureau and takes out liquor and then goes to refrigerator and takes out bowl of cubes and drops some into glasses. He doesn't turn toward Bernadette as he gives his next speech*)

KENNY: You work for some sort of agency, don't you?

BERNADETTE: Scripts.

KENNY (*Turning*) *Scene!* (*Acting it out*) Nice young girl comes to pick up her affianced. To go out drape buying. He is gone. But in the apartment is his roommate. A rat. (*Aside*) I am a rat, you know that, don't you, Bernadette.

BERNADETTE: So I've been informed.

KENNY: (*Play-acting*) A compulsive sexual maniac. Guided only by his animal instincts. *Question*: Will the rat attempt to make the fiancée of his best friend on the evening of their wedding? Tune in tomorrow, dear friends. (*Hands drink to Bernadette*) I can't get over it. A girl like you, a knock-out, and a guy like Frank gets you.

BERNADETTE: He's a fine man; he'll make a wonderful father.

KENNY: (*Directly*) Is that all you Catholic girls want in a man, a wonderful father?

BERNADETTE: Why, no . . .

KENNY: Don't you care . . . or want a man who can make love? (*Bernadette puts down her drink and rises*)

KENNY: (*Acting*) *Wait!* Don't turn that knob! Will the rat continue in this vein. Will there be any sense of decency rising in him to turn him off his course. He has known so few nice girls. All have yielded. To his charm. To his approach. To his sense of knowing the right approach in every situation. He's a rat, friends of the audience. He knows it. The girl knows it. But he's a man and the girl is doomed to a "nice" boy who'll make a good husband, impregnating her dutifully at the recommended intervals. (*Bernadette turns from Kenny. He goes to her*)

KENNY: Look at me, Bernadette. Frank bores you stiff. Admit it. You'd swap him in a moment if a real man came along.

BERNADETTE: (*Turning to him*) Your imagination is exceeded only by your vulgarity. (*Bernadette starts right. Kenny crosses in her path*)

KENNY: *Scene!* The nice young girl attempts to leave as she properly should. But the rat jumps in her path. Out of habit he wishes to ruin her. (*Directly*) Go on, marry the jerk. But aren't you entitled, isn't every girl entitled to one terrific experience before she settles down to . . . (*Bernadette begins crossing again. As she attempts to go around Kenny, he grabs her by the wrist*)

KENNY: *Scene!* Violence. Will the rat rape her!

BERNADETTE: Please, you're hurting me.

KENNY: Please, please, please. You'll like it and I need it so.

BERNADETTE: (*Struggling*) I'll scream . . . (*Kenny quickly cups his hand across her mouth as he locks her to him with the same arm*)

KENNY: (*Feverishly*) Just once you'll see what a man is like. You'll love it, baby, I promise. Oh baby, baby. (*With his free hand, Kenny begins ripping Bernadette's blouse*)

KENNY: And you want me. You want me. I sense it. You want me to take you. You want it, you want it. (*Bernadette breaks away from Kenny and steps right. Kenny takes a step toward Bernadette who turns and slaps him hard across the face. Kenny stands stunned for a moment before speaking*)

KENNY: I want you. Very much . . . (*Bernadette grabs her purse off chair and turns to Kenny. She attempts to think of something vile enough to say, but can't, so she looks at him a moment and then leaves. Kenny stands for a moment stunned, then takes out address book and walks toward the phone*)

KENNY: *Scene!* The nice girl has escaped. The rat takes out his telephone book. He walks to the phone (*Which he does*) He looks through it for a number. (*Which he does*) He begins dialing. (*Which he does*) But before completing his call, he stops and lets the receiver hang loosely in his hand. (*Which he does*) Cold. Empty. His just dessert. Rejected. Unwanted. (*Slowly the door opens and Bernadette enters and just stands. Kenny turns slowly and looks at her as the lights dim slowly out*)

THE END

THE MAD PROFESSOR

THE MAD PROFESSOR

CHARACTERS

THE PROFESSOR
THE COLLEAGUE
THE WAITER

Setting: A room in a restaurant
Time: The present or the past

THE MAD PROFESSOR

(The scene is a table in a restaurant. The two men are sitting at the table).

COLLEAGUE: But, my dear colleague, how is it possible, if you are mad as you say, that you are able to continue at the university where one of the regulations specifically prohibits the continuance in employment of professors who have become mad. *(The Professor is about to answer when the Waiter enters with chocolate which he places before the two men. The Waiter leaves)*

PROFESSOR: Very simple. I myself noticed that some of my actions seemed irrational. So I made a thorough study of my behavior.

COLLEAGUE: (*Repeating*) You made a thorough study of your behavior.

PROFESSOR: Yes. Using all my training in logic, I was forced to come to the conclusion that I was mad. Quite mad.

COLLEAGUE: (*Repeating*) Quite mad.

PROFESSOR: Thus, since logic could no longer be an ally, I forsook it and was forced to turn to cleverness.

COLLEAGUE: Cleverness. And what did you do, Professor?

PROFESSOR: I immediately confided in certain members of my department that I was mad. There are in every department those who immediately spread every bit of news and gossip and rumor to other members of the department. To these I confided that I was mad.

COLLEAGUE: That you were mad.

PROFESSOR: Yes, and then, as an extra measure, I did things that only a mad man would do. I did these purposely.

COLLEAGUE: Not because you were mad, but because you wanted them to think you were mad.

PROFESSOR: That is correct.

COLLEAGUE: And whispering to everyone that you *were* mad.

PROFESSOR: That is correct.

COLLEAGUE: And because you told everyone you were mad when the question arose as to your madness the only response was laughter.

PROFESSOR: The only response was laughter.

COLLEAGUE: So there would be no investigation regarding your madness.

PROFESSOR: Madness.

COLLEAGUE: How clever! A madman could not be so clever.

PROFESSOR: Wrong! A mad man can be very clever.

COLLEAGUE: I do not believe that you are mad.

PROFESSOR: But I am.

COLLEAGUE: We will talk no more on the topic. This is simply a humor.

PROFESSOR: I *am* mad. I admit it. All the evidence testifies to it.

COLLEAGUE: A humor simply. And besides, one cannot be contentedly mad unless one has a private income.

PROFESSOR: I have a private income. Rather large.

COLLEAGUE: My wife and I are entertaining Saturday night. Will you honor us with your presence.

PROFESSOR: Of course.

COLLEAGUE: More chocolate? (*The Professor nods and the Colleague pours more chocolate as the lights dim*)

END

THE DRY CLEANER'S BOY

THE DRY CLEANER'S BOY

CHARACTERS

JIM, a white boy
GEORGE, his lover

Setting: Jim's apartment in Atlanta
Time: The present

THE DRY CLEANER'S BOY

(The scene opens on living room of Jim's two room apartment in Atlanta. Jim, a white boy in his middle twenties, sits at table center sipping coffee and glancing at a newspaper he has in front of him. He wears shirt, tie, etc., but no coat).

JIM: (*Glancing at watch*) Hey, George, you'll be late for the office (*There is the sound of an electric razor off-stage left*)

GEORGE: (*His voice coming from offstage left*) Three minutes more.

JIM: (*After pause*) Thanks, George, for last night.

GEORGE: (*Over noise of razor*) And thank you, Jim.

JIM: You were pretty wonderful, you know.

GEORGE: Not bad yourself.

JIM: Did I hurt you, George?

GEORGE: Why do you ask?

JIM: You were pretty tight.

GEORGE: Don't do *that* very often. (*Jim takes another sip of coffee and looks at paper*)

JIM: Will you come here again, George?

GEORGE: If you want me to.

JIM: I want you to. (*Pause*) George, did you work out with weights.

GEORGE: A couple years ago. Should I start again?

JIM: No, you're just right. (*Pause*) George, should I work out with weights?

GEORGE: No, I like you as you are.

JIM: You slept last night didn't you?

GEORGE: A little.

JIM: I didn't.

GEORGE: I'm sorry.

JIM: You excite me too much.

GEORGE: That will pass.

JIM: Think so?

GEORGE: And then you won't want me coming again.

JIM: Never happen.

GEORGE: I like coming here, Jim. I want to come even after we're tired of sex with one another. Jim, what are your interests? Art?

JIM: I know the terminology but have no feeling.

GEORGE: Theatre?

JIM: Don't understand it.

GEORGE: Music?

JIM: Yes.

GEORGE: Hayden?

JIM: Very much.

GEORGE: I have records. I'll bring them. We'll play them and I'll cook for you, Jim.

JIM: I like plain food, but subtly spiced.

GEORGE: My grandmother taught me how to use spices (*Jim looks at his watch*)

JIM: George, you'll be late for the office.

GEORGE: On my way now. (*George steps through entranceway. He is a Negro in his early twenties and is stripped to the waist. He puts on his shirt*)

JIM: (*Good-naturedly*) For Christ's sake, George, put on your shirt before I drag you off to bed again.

GEORGE: (*Teasing*) I'd like that.

JIM: And we'd both lose our jobs for being late. No thanks. (*Jim gets up and puts on his coat. George quickly puts on tie and his coat and they start for the door right*)

JIM: George, can you make it Tuesday.

GEORGE: After work? After dark? (*Jim nods*)

GEORGE: Yes, I can make it. (*Jim turns to door*)

GEORGE: Jim.

JIM: Yes.

GEORGE: I came in the dark. It's light now. Nine o'clock in the morning. Morning in a large apartment house. Morning in Atlanta. (*Jim understands. He crosses left over to closet and takes out a pair of pants. He hands them to George*)

JIM: (*Gaily*) You're the Dry Cleaner's Boy. (*George walks left and stands behind Jim*)

GEORGE: Who walks three feet behind. (*George measures the three feet and stands behind Jim. Jim starts toward door, but turns, goes to George, spreads his arms apart, and embraces and kisses him. He then turns, measures the three feet, walks and turns*)

JIM: Tuesday?

GEORGE: Tuesday. (*Jim winks at George. George winks back and they exit, George being careful to remain three feet behind Jim*)

END

THE HOURGLASS

THE HOURGLASS

CHARACTERS

MME. PAULA DE TAUSSIN, a widow in her early forties
MARIE, her maid
EMILE, her masculine friend

Setting: The Paris Salon of Mme. de Taussin
Time: Late summer, 1888

THE HOURGLASS

(The setting is the salon of Mme. de Taussin. Center stage there is a love seat. To the left of this seat there is a table upon which is seen a rather large, conspicuous hourglass. The other furniture about the room balances this center arrangement. There is a door off right which leads into a hallway. The door off left leads into Paula's private quarters. After the curtains have parted, Marie enters from door right. MARIE is in her fifties, a homely large household maid. She is knowing, yet sympathetic in her worldly French way. Marie crosses left)

MARIE: (*Calling*) Madame Paula. (*At doorway left*) Madame Paula.

PAULA: (*From within*) Yes, Marie?

MARIE: Your gentleman has arrived.

PAULA: (*From within*) Monsieur Emile?

MARIE: Yes, Madame.

PAULA: (*From within*) Delay him a moment, Marie, then have him enter.

MARIE: Into the salon?

PAULA: (*From within*) Yes, into the salon (*Entering through door left*) As usual. (*PAULA is an attractive woman in her early forties. She has a beautiful figure and a gracious manner. There is a softness about her which is greatly appealing. As Paula enters, Marie turns to exit right. At right doorway she turns*)

MARIE: Madame . . .

PAULA: Yes, Marie, what is it?

MARIE: I . . . Oh, nothing, Madame . . .

PAULA: You've something on your mind. Come, Marie, we're old friends, aren't we?

MARIE: Yes, Madame.

PAULA: Then, speak out.

MARIE: Well, this gentleman . . .

PAULA: Monsieur Emile . . .

MARIE: Yes. Madame, I . . . like him.

PAULA: And so do I.

MARIE: (*Hopefully*) I hope he visits often.

PAULA: Perhaps he will.

MARIE: We thought that about the others.

PAULA: (*Annoyed*) *Others?*

MARIE: Begging your pardon, Madame. I'll show Monsieur Emile in. (*Marie exits right. Paula looks around the room and then at the hourglass. She notices a speck of dust on the glass. Frowning, she crosses, takes out her handkerchief, and wipes the speck from the glass. She then turns and faces door right. Marie reenters with Emile, then exits left. EMILE is a pleasant looking man in his early thirties. There is an air of conquest about him. He crosses over to Paula and kisses her hand*)

EMILE: Madame de Taussin.

PAULA: Emile, how kind of you to come.

EMILE: The kindness, Madame, was all yours. In asking me to visit you. (*Emile steps right and looks about the room*)

PAULA: Do you like my salon?

EMILE: Indeed!

PAULA: This is my favorite room. It was also the favorite room of my late husband.

EMILE: (*Politely*) Indeed?

PAULA: The colors are so warm. And the furniture in such good taste. (*Pointing*) This love seat, for example. So inviting.

EMILE: (*Softly*) Indeed.

PAULA: My late husband decorated this room.

EMILE: Oh?

PAULA: Henri had such good taste. In everything. (*Emile looks at Paula knowingly, then nods politely. Paula crosses left of table*)

PAULA: For months after our marriage, we combed all of Paris. Henri was so particular that a year passed before we completely furnished the house.

EMILE: (*Noticing*) What an extraordinary hourglass. Where did your husband find *that?*

PAULA: He didn't. That came *after* his death. The only thing *I* have added to our domicile. (*Walks right behind sofa and points*) Come, Emile, sit down.

EMILE: With pleasure, Madame de Taussin. (*Emile sits*)

PAULA: Paula.

EMILE: (*Smiling*) Paula. Come, join me. (*Paula smiles, then crosses to table left. She turns the hourglass*)

EMILE: Why did you do that?

PAULA: When the sand no longer flows, then you must leave.

EMILE: La Madame du Sablier. The Lady of the Hourglass. (*Paula smiles in enjoyment*)

EMILE: That's what they call you here in Paris. Now, I know why. (*Paula crosses left down behind table*)

PAULA: (*Repeating*) La Madame du Sablier.

EMILE: How fortunate it was that we met again last night at the opera.

PAULA: *Fortunate* or deliberate?

EMILE: Deliberate. Meeting you three different times this past week was no accident.

PAULA: How did you . . .

EMILE: I simply followed your carriage evenings.

PAULA: Delightful!

EMILE: But come, sit here with me.

PAULA: (*Raising finger teasingly*) If I do, you will probably want to make love.

EMILE: Isn't that why I was invited?

PAULA: (*Simply*) Yes.

EMILE: (*Noticing hourglass*) Time wastes away. (*Paula crosses right and sits on left side of seat. Emile turns toward her. His line of vision hits the hourglass. Emile takes Paula's hand and kisses it*)

EMILE: How delicate your hands are. So white.

PAULA: Henri said they reminded him of snow-colored doves. (*Emile takes one of her hands and places it against his cheek*)

EMILE: And soft as doves' feathers. Why, Paula, you tremble!

PAULA: Yes.

EMILE: Why? Are you afraid of me?

PAULA: No, not at all. It's . . . Henri.

EMILE: But your husband is dead.

PAULA: Yes. All those years I was so afraid of him. I cannot realize that I am now free.

(Emile kisses Paula's hand again, then he takes her wrist and kisses that. Then, he edges closer to Paula and kisses her on the throat)

PAULA: Henri was always so jealous. And for no reason. For fifteen years I was faithful to him. But he was everlastingly suspicious. He was suspicious of anyone who even looked at me.

EMILE: You're so beautiful. (*Again Emile kisses her throat*)

PAULA: Never in those fifteen years did I have a moment's rest. His anger. My weeping. Always an emotional turmoil.

EMILE: He's gone.

PAULA: Yes, Henri is gone.

EMILE: And now you have peace.

PAULA: Yes, now everything is peaceful. (*Emile kisses Paula behind her ear*)

EMILE: The empty years are gone, my darling. Today all Paris is at your feet.

PAULA: Yes. Today, I may have anyone. (*Emile kisses Paula on the cheek*)

EMILE: All those years of pent-up passion, they're yours to unleash. With me, Paula. With me.

PAULA: (*Sighing*) With someone.

EMILE: How delicate your nose is, and how limpid your eyes.

PAULA: Often, after Henri's accusations, I swore that I would have many lovers following his death.

EMILE: You need only one. Paula, take me.

PAULA: I vowed I would take a lover for every accusation.

EMILE: (*Softly*) Cast off the wasted years. This moment is the only thing of importance.

PAULA: (*Noticing*) I am no longer trembling.

EMILE: I am the man for you. Paula, you must love me.

PAULA: Love?

EMILE: Come into my arms and we'll forget *him.*

PAULA: Forget Henri? No, he'll never be forgotten. His spirit will live as long as I live.

EMILE: Think no more of your husband, Paula. He is buried and in his grave.

PAULA: No, he is not buried. (*Emile looks up questioningly*)

PAULA: I had the body cremated.

EMILE: And the ashes?

PAULA: There (*Paula points to the hourglass*)

EMILE: In the hourglass?

PAULA: Yes. You see, I have put Henri to use. He times my love affairs. (*Turning right*) Come, Emile, let us continue. . . . (*Emile is flustered a bit, but bends over to kiss Paula. His gaze, however, is still on the hourglass*)

PAULA: Why do you hesitate? (*Teasingly*) Do you not *burn* with passion?

EMILE: Of course, Paula, but it's . . .

PAULA: It's what? (*Emile hesitates a moment, then picks up Paula's hand and kisses it hurriedly*)

EMILE: I've suddenly remembered something.

PAULA: But what, dear Emile?

EMILE: A wretched appointment. I must leave. You'll forgive me?

PAULA: Of course, Emile. There'll be other times.

EMILE: My dearest Paula.

(*Again Emile kisses Paula's hand, then rises and starts right. At the door he turns and bows to Paula. After a hasty glance at the hourglass, he frowns and exits. After a moment, Marie enters from left*)

MARIE: Oh, Madame! And he was so nice!

PAULA: They are *all so nice.*

MARIE: Soon there'll be no more to invite. Madame, this is *madness.* Find a man and love him. Forget Henri.

PAULA: Dear Marie, how you scold me.

MARIE: And how little my scolding matters. I cannot understand. Since your husband's death, it seems that is *you* who no longer lives. (*Marie mutters to herself and exits left. Paula rises and circles behind the seat to follow Marie. She then turns, crosses to the hourglass, and touches it tenderly*)

PAULA: Oh, Henri, will I never stop . . . loving you? (*Paula sighs, turns, and exits left. The stage is empty for a moment, then the curtains slowly close*)

THE END

THE BRONZE STATUE

THE BRONZE STATUE

CHARACTERS

GEORGE SZOLD, nephew of the late John Szold
IRVING ARMSTRONG, his friend

Place: Boston studio of the late John Szold
Time: Afternoon, the present

THE BRONZE STATUE

(The scene opens on the studio of the late famous sculptor, John Szold. There is a barenness about the room. Packing boxes are placed carelessly about. There is a table and chair down left. A bureau is upstage right. Downstage right is a table and chair. In the center of the room is a large wooden box in which a statue is placed. The contents of the box are not visible to the audience. To the right of the box stands GEORGE SZOLD, a man in his middle thirties. He has a plank in one hand and a hammer and some nails in the other. He stands looking into the box. After a moment, he puts the plank at stage right and crosses to table downstage left and places his finger into a pot which is on a small electric stove. He withdraws his finger and frowns. He again crosses over to the box, looks at its contents, and then calls to someone in the adjoining room left).

GEORGE: Oh, Irv.

IRVIN: (*From adjoining room*) Yes?

GEORGE: Last chance to see the statue before I nail on the back planks.

IRVIN: (*From adjoining room*) O.K. (*A moment later Irvin enters from left. IRVIN is about the same age as George. George crosses right*)

IRVIN: Are you sorry you've sold it?

GEORGE: *The Youth of Bronze?* No, I think not. It will help pay off Uncle John's debts. Poor Uncle. His sculptures in galleries all over the world. Yet practically a bankrupt at his death. (*George steps right and picks up board and nails*)

GEORGE: Say, Irv, how's about checking the water while I hammer up this board. (*Irvin crosses left and checks water. George hammers on one of the planks*)

IRVIN: Boiling!

GEORGE: Good. (*Pointing to bureau right*) There're some tea bags in that first drawer over there. The drawer sticks a little, so give it a good pull. (*Irvin crosses right and pulls out the drawer. It drops to the floor. Some letters are sealed on the back of the drawer with adhesive tape*)

IRVIN: Hello!

GEORGE: What's the matter?

IRVIN: There's a packet of envelopes secured to the back of the drawer.

GEORGE: Let's see. (*George removes the envelopes and examines them. Irvin replaces drawer*)

GEORGE: Uncle's writing. I guess something he wanted hidden.

IRVIN: Ah ha! The family skeletons begin to rattle.

GEORGE (*Smiling*) No, I'm afraid not. Uncle John was a very harmless old man. (*Looking at envelopes*) These envelopes on top are addressed to a Lance Cooper. *Lance Cooper.*

IRVIN: Why the frown?

GEORGE: Lance Cooper was the one who modelled for this statue. Twenty years ago.

IRVIN: Judging from the sculpture, he must have been a very handsome lad.

GEORGE: There was always a mystery about the fellow. He and Uncle were very good friends. One day there was an item in the newspaper about the boy's disappearance. A long search was made, but nothing ever turned up. (*Irvin steps down right near George*)

IRVIN: How did your uncle take it?

GEORGE: Mother said he acted very strangely—locked himself up for weeks at a time—not speaking to anyone. Uncle cast this last statue himself instead of sending it out to the foundry. Then, when it was finished, he just withdrew from the world, and spent his last twenty years here alone in this studio.

IRVIN: Let's read the letters, George. Maybe after all this time . . .

GEORGE: (*Frowning*) Irv, I think I'd rather not read them.

IRVIN: What!

GEORGE: The past is dead. Along with Uncle John. I have a feeling I should burn these letters, *whatever* they are. . . .

IRVIN: Say look, George. Not only was John Szold your uncle, but he was one of the world's greatest sculptors. It'd be like . . . burning letters written by Shakespeare.

GEORGE: I guess you're right. And maybe there's something here that'd clear up the mystery, yet surely Uncle would have done whatever he could twenty years ago. (*Looking at letters*) Here are some written to Uncle with the initials L.C. up in the corner.

IRVIN: Put them in order, and let's see how they read.

GEORGE: O.K. They're all dated within a few days of one another. Here's an envelope with only clippings.

IRVIN: Clippings?

GEORGE: About the disappearance of Lance Cooper. Dated September 20, 1924.

IRVIN: When are the letters dated?

GEORGE: The first is from Uncle to Cooper, September 1, 1924, and the last dated September 18, 1924, also from Uncle to the boy.

IRVIN: That's just two days before his disappearance. Any letters *after* the 20th?

GEORGE: No. Just more clippings saying the search had been abandoned. In these first letters, there seems to be some sort of an argument going on—nothing worth quoting. Let's see, here's one dated September 15, from Uncle to Cooper.

IRVIN: Read it.

GEORGE: O.K. (*Smiling*) But if any skeletons rattle, kindly disregard same.

IRVIN: Fire away!

GEORGE: (*Reading*) My dear Lance: You are killing me. (*George suddenly becomes sober and his voice changes as he continues reading*) This torment by you cannot go on much longer. I have given you everything. What else is there left. Have you no pity, no compassion? I beg of you to return. I forgive you your indiscretions. Please, Lance, return. Signed: J.S.

IRVIN: (*After pause*) Well, what do you make of that?

GEORGE: I . . . I can't believe . . .

IRVIN: Is there any kind of a reply?

GEORGE: Yes. The last letter here from Cooper. (*Reading*) Dear Mr. Szold. The bank informs me that our joint account is overdrawn. Why have you been so careless about this matter? Don't you realize the embarrassment it causes me? I trust you will take care of this situation immediately. Signed: Lance.

IRVIN: Say, the plot *really* thickens!

GEORGE: Here's Uncle's answer. (*Reading*) My dear Lance: This is the last letter you will receive from me. Everything I have is yours, you know that. Without your companionship there is nothing. Come to my studio tomorrow afternoon at three and I will make final arrangements. After tomorrow you need not see me again ever. Yet I shall always go on seeing you. Come, my dear Lance, and I shall make you eternal.

IRVIN: What do you know!

GEORGE: Strange. . . .

IRVIN: (*Crossing left*) "And I shall make you eternal. . . ." (*Turning right to George*) Why, George, do you know what happened!

GEORGE: (*Sharply*) Irv, don't say it!

IRVIN: (*Quickly*) I must! Lance Cooper came here that afternoon: (*George quickly turns and goes back to look at the statue. Irvin joins him*)

IRVIN: The only statue he cast himself.

GEORGE: It can't be possible. (*George crosses to table downstage right, takes out lighter, and sets it aflame*)

IRVING: (*Crossing right*) What are you doing? (*Without answering, George sets fire to the letters and watches them burn*)

IRVIN: But people should know, George. The boy's family.

GEORGE: (*Quickly*) Imagination. That's all it is. Our imagination.

IRVIN: The statue needn't be wrecked. Just one part . . .

GEORGE: (*Quickly*) It couldn't be sold then. (*Pause*) Besides, things like this don't happen, Irvin. Do you *understand,* Irvin? (*Irvin crosses left. George turns, crosses left to box, and quickly begins hammering up the remaining plank. Irvin collapses in chair at table left*)

IRVIN: (*Pleading*) God, George, what'll we do. What'll we do?

GEORGE: (*Stepping down right*) Nothing. Nothing at all. Uncle John's bronze statue no longer belongs to us, but . . . to eternity. (*Both men look at the box almost as if hypnotized as the curtains slowly close*)

THE END

STILLBIRTH

STILLBIRTH

CHARACTERS

UNBORN GIRL CHARACTER
UNBORN BOY CHARACTER
PLAYWRIGHT

Setting: Empty stage in an empty theatre
Time: Midnight, the present

STILLBIRTH

(The play takes place on a darkened stage, empty except for table, chairs and miscellaneous props. The UNBORN GIRL CHARACTER is dressed in a black T-shirt and black skirt. The UNBORN BOY CHARACTER wears a black T-shirt and black slacks. Both wear black eye masks. As the curtains part, the two unborn characters are sitting at the table)

GIRL: Do you think the master'll be back?

BOY: Yes, I suppose so, but frankly, I'm so sick and tired of his stormings and rantings I'd just as soon go back to that vacuum he *calls* his brain and not be born a story character at all.

GIRL: I *wonder* if humans have so much trouble being born?

BOY: Oh no, all *their* trouble comes after birth. It's different with us characters. Once we're born, either in a play or a story, all of our troubles are over.

GIRL: Yes, once we're born. But it's such a wearisome process I wonder if it's worth all the trouble.

BOY: We'll probably both end up as abortions.

GIRL: That's a possibility. (*Stands, crosses left*) I try to be philosophical about everything. Really, a vacuum is quite comfortable. Nothing pleasant happens, but then nothing unpleasant happens, so things even out. It's the same way with human beings, I guess. They all get to be born, but they all have to die, so things even themselves out.

BOY: You stole that line from one of our master's plays, didn't you?

GIRL: Yes, the one called *Ex Libris*. I was in it for a while, but then the boss decided there were too many characters so he stuck me back on the shelf. I didn't mind because the play was very bad.

BOY: He thought about my being in it too for awhile. I was scared to death he would use me. I hoped he'd save me for one of his better plays, a new comedy, perhaps, but I'm afraid now he's gone mad. Completely mad.

GIRL: (*Turning right*) You're right there. Mad as a hatter. That's why I don't even want to appear in this new play. This crazy thing about essences. It'll be such a *mad* collection of thoughts that *no one* will care to be in it or to see it. That's just what Miss Carlyle, the actress, told him. She said he was mad and he said she was late for rehearsal which was a *much* worse offense in the theatre.

BOY: I like Miss Carlyle.

GIRL: I shall be *she* if this madman ever finishes his crazy play (*Turning left*) I shall be beautiful and dazzling. Then it won't matter what crazy speeches master puts into my mouth. People won't be listening and whenever I come to a particularly dull speech I'll wink and pull my shoulder in just a little bit. That will help push the play along to a more exciting spot.

BOY: (*Rising*) Oh, but wouldn't the boss want to kill you for that!

GIRL: Shh, I feel him coming down the corridor outside. He'll open the back door in a minute and then come up to the stage all a-blowing and puffing. I hope he doesn't work with us too long tonight. I'm simply fagged. (*Girl crosses right and sits*)

BOY: So am I. (*Sits*) He's been in such a rotten mood all day long no one can work with him. Mad. Yes, he's gone mad. That's all there is to it!

GIRL: Shh. Here he comes. (*Through the back door of the auditorium enters the angry playwright with a flashlight in his hand. As to his physical appearance, he can look like anyone who wants to act the part. Without noticing the audience, he grimly walks down the aisle and onto the stage. Once on the stage he looks around, then exits right for a moment and then comes back on*)

PLAYWRIGHT: (*Calling*) Charlie. Oh, Charlie. (*There is no answer*)

PLAYWRIGHT: Oh, Charlie!

GIRL: He went home.

PLAYWRIGHT: What!

BOY: He was angry because you swore at him.

GIRL: Yes. He's a sensitive soul.

PLAYWRIGHT: But I've got to have some lights.

BOY: He locked up everything and went home to sulk. He said you didn't appreciate what a sensitive artist he is.

PLAYWRIGHT: Hah! He's about as sensitive as a wet bag of cement. I suppose when he left he told that tribe of morons who *call* themselves stagehands they could all go home.

GIRL: Yes sir.

PLAYWRIGHT: Well, I don't care. In fact I'm glad. I'll show those nincumpoops just how much I need them. If a play's any good, it doesn't need a lot of fancy sets for a bunch of numbskulls to put in the wrong places at the wrong time. (*Crosses left behind table*) I'll just use a cyclorama. I'll put it in place myself before the show to make sure it's right.

BOY: What about lights?

PLAYWRIGHT: I won't have any! That electrician prima donna thinks the sun rises and sets on him. Just because he *sometimes* clicks the proper switches on and off when it's written *that* way in the prompt book. Well, this play will be performed in the dark. I'll set it at night.

GIRL: No light at all in the whole play?

PLAYWRIGHT: Well, if it's a moonlit night, I'll punch a hole in the ceiling and let some light stream down. That'll give a dandy effect. Better than any these imbeciles around here could dream up with *all* their equipment!

BOY: No sets. No lights.

GIRL: But how will they see that *beautiful* costume Mme. Duprea is designing?

PLAYWRIGHT: You mean the thing with all the sequins?

GIRL: Oh yes. It will simply dazzle everyone.

PLAYWRIGHT: We're not using it.

GIRL: Not using it!

PLAYWRIGHT: No. It's too glittering. It will interfere with

the play. I told that French seamstress to take off every one of the sequins and to dye the material to black or gray.

GIRL: Oh, no!

PLAYWRIGHT: She wouldn't do it, so I gave her the sack. Told her we'd get along without costumes. (*Stepping right*) I shall drape all my characters in black. I don't *want* any flashy costumes competing with what *I* have to say in the play. That was the trouble with my last play. Beautiful lines, but no one heard them. All through the performance they were looking at the spectacular sets, or they were admiring the gorgeous costumes, or they were hypnotized by the lights which changed every twenty seconds for no reason at all.

BOY: No sets, no lights, no costumes. What a play!

PLAYWRIGHT: I've even been thinking of kicking out the actors. What a pestilent tribe of egocentrics! All they want is comedy roles. None of them have an *essence* in them.

BOY: But how could you do a play without actors?

PLAYWRIGHT: There must be a way. (*Stepping left*) Perhaps with marionettes. Or maybe I could use shadows—but then, I'll have no lights. I guess I'll *have* to have actors. But I shall choose them carefully. They must be free from any ideas of their own. They should be completely mechanical, and obey me implicitly. They must realize they're just *mechanisms* for expressing my dialogue.

BOY: You told Mr. Davis in rehearsal last night that he was *too* mechanical.

PLAYWRIGHT: Well, he was. I want my actors to be mechanical without seeming to be mechanical. Davis isn't too bad in rehearsals, but when he gets before an audience he loses his mind. All of these actors do. Blast 'em.

BOY: Well, anyway, master, you gotta have an audience.

PLAYWRIGHT: (*Crossing right in front of table*) Yes, therein lies the evil of this whole damned business. What great plays I could produce if it weren't for those chattering fingledejigs sitting out there, squirming in their seats, coughing and sneezing. That's the worst. That sneezing! Here my actors have worked up a beautiful scene of suspense, and just before they reach their peak, someone in the audience . . . sneezes. I should like to stand at the entranceway and keep out every person who looked like he might be a sneezer. And I'd keep out the wrigglers. And I'd forbid entrance to any of these people who think it's so clever to whisper during the play and make pleasant witticisms. Yes, how wonderful it would be if the playwright didn't have to put up with an audience.

GIRL: It's getting late, master. Shouldn't we begin the play?

PLAYWRIGHT: Good idea. I want to start it from the very beginning. Save only the best speeches.

BOY: Have you thought about the names we're to have?

GIRL: Yes, master, it would save a lot of confusion.

PLAYWRIGHT: No, I haven't decided yet. The play's symbolic so I can't use just ordinary names. You there, character, you're to be the essence of girlhood, and you, you're to be the essence of boyhood.

BOY: Is that all we're to be—just essences?

PLAYWRIGHT: That's all. Just essences. It's to be my greatest play. (*Crosses left to behind table*) I want to capture the spirit of boyhood and girlhood without any of its fancy frills. There must be a sheerness in the play. Yes, it must be sheer sheer and nothing else. No personalities, no clash, just essence. Sheer sheer. Do you understand?

GIRL: Frankly, master, I wish you would save me for your next play. A comedy, perhaps.

PLAYWRIGHT: What!

GIRL: You know the one that's going to be so funny. The one where all these girls are after this one fellow and he has to hide in my boudoir because . . .

PLAYWRIGHT: (*Crossing left*) My dear character, you don't seem to realize what I'm doing for you. All these years I've been saving you for this play. Now the play is being written. *Anyone* can write comedies or melodramas, but I am writing pure essence. Can't you understand?

GIRL: I'd still rather be in that comedy and have Herbert or whatever you will call him hide in my *boudoir*.

PLAYWRIGHT: That play will probably never be written.

BOY: What! I've got some wonderful lines just swell for the situation.

PLAYWRIGHT: That's the trouble. It's a situation. Another hack situation. Been done a million times. Why do it again?

BOY: But boss, it's what the audiences want.

PLAYWRIGHT: That's because they don't know about anything else. Wait until I've given them essence. Sheer sheer. Now, let's not waste any more time. (*Visualizing*) The setting will be a deserted heath. It is midnight. Dark and eerie. A trace of wind perhaps. You, essence of girlhood, will be here waiting for essence of boyhood.

GIRL: Oh, I understand. I'm here on a heath waiting for my boy friend who's stood me up maybe?

PLAYWRIGHT: No, no, no! Can't you understand? I want none of the ordinary problems. Just the essence. (*Visualizing*) Your soul is lying there on the grass of the heath. Only the stars look down upon it.

GIRL: I thought it was going to be all dark.

PLAYWRIGHT: Well, it can be dark with stars, can't it?

GIRL: Yeah, I guess so.

PLAYWRIGHT: And don't "yeah" me. You're not a human, so don't talk like one.

GIRL: If I ain't gonna talk like a human, how will the audience understand me.

PLAYWRIGHT: I don't *want* them to understand you. I just want them to feel you. There must be a transmission of essence. That's what I'm working for. We're here on the heath. Girlhood and boyhood. The essence, that's all. I'll write you beautiful speeches. I've some already written here in my pockets. You'll both be standing and saying these speeches to one another. They probably won't make sense at first because they're . . . essence.

GIRL: Sheer sheer.

PLAYWRIGHT: That's right. And there's to be no moving around. No moving at all to distract the audience.

BOY: I gotta move to enter if I ain't on the heath at the opening.

PLAYWRIGHT: (*Crossing right to behind table*) Yes, that is a problem I'll have to work on.

GIRL: But master, won't the audience expect a little action of some kind? I mean, a boy and a girl alone, together, out on a deserted heath.

PLAYWRIGHT: You have an evil mind. Remember the characters in this play are to be essences. Just essences.

GIRL: O.K. Slip me a speech.

PLAYWRIGHT: (*Crossing right*) The play will open with you alone on the heath. You will stand with your arms reaching toward the stars. After a moment, you will seem to whisper "Breathe in, breath out, . . . oh mighty infinite. Oh, nothingness which is everything, oh everything which is nothingness. Breathe in, breathe out, oh short-lived infinite."

GIRL: (*After pause*) That's what I gotta say?

PLAYWRIGHT: Oh, there's more. It'll make me immortal. How lucky you characters are that you're to be in it. You'll live on and on forever. Coming to life every time the play is presented or read. Yes, this flesh of mine will crumble, decay, and rot away, but I shall live on because of *you*. Your immortality will be but a shadowy reflection of my own.

BOY: I'd still rather be in that comedy.

PLAYWRIGHT: *What!* That comedy will last only a season and then die. This play will live forever because of its *essence*. You can't kill *essence*.

GIRL: No, but you can kill audiences *giving* 'em that stuff.

PLAYWRIGHT: How dare you! Don't you recognize poetic creation? I expected the *others* not to understand, but you, why you're part of me. (*Turning left*) My brain, my mind, my very soul. (*Turning out*) Oh God, I wonder if Byron, Keats, Shelley, and the others were plagued with such tormentors?

BOY: Look boss, in that comedy you were thinking about last month, remember the second act ending that's had you so worried? Well, if I could disguise myself as the girl's aunt, it'd be hilarious.

PLAYWRIGHT: The second act?

BOY: Yeah, that'd give it the punch it needs. The third act's already blocked out, ain't it? Why, it'll run for two years. Maybe longer.

PLAYWRIGHT: Yes, *all* my comedies are successes. For just about two years each.

GIRL: What're ya griping about?

PLAYWRIGHT: I want to write a play which will flop. (*Idealistically*) Flop because it's a hundred years ahead of its time.

GIRL: Well, that'd be a *new* excuse for a flop.

PLAYWRIGHT: No one in the theatre has ever dared to present just essence. *Essence. Sheer sheer.* What's at the core of everything we do, everything which exists? Essence. Everything else is façade. Covering. Artificality.

BOY: Sounds great, boss. But let's be practical. When this boy essence meets this girl essence, what happens?

PLAYWRIGHT: Why, the greatest thing possible. The glorious inevitable. The *climax* of my play.

GIRL: What happens?

PLAYWRIGHT: Why, there's a union of essences.

GIRL: The cops will never let you do it.

BOY: We could try.

PLAYWRIGHT: (*Indignantly*) It's a spiritual union! The essences unite and the world dissolves into the starry essence of the infinite.

BOY: Gee, boss, you gotta have stagehands for that ending!

GIRL: I don't like it!

PLAYWRIGHT: What!

GIRL: (*Rising*) I don't like it. I refuse to be in that play. It's a terrible idea. I shan't be in it!

BOY: (*Rising*) I don't want to be in it either, boss.

PLAYWRIGHT: I can't believe it. My own characters deserting! I can understand the electricians and the stagehands quitting. And I can understand the actors leaving. Shallow people without poetic souls. All of them. But you. You're the best of me inside.

GIRL: That new comedy or nothing.

BOY: Same here, boss.

PLAYWRIGHT: But it'll only run a year, then you'll die.

GIRL: But what a year! Sixteen costume changes. With flashing sequins on every one.

BOY: And four big sets. All done up in purple and yellow with orange and black spots. What a show!

PLAYWRIGHT: You have no right to desert me this way. All these years I've been saving you for my essence play. You'll live forever.

BOY: Nuts!

PLAYWRIGHT: I *refuse* to do that comedy. You can't talk me into it. You've been listening to the others. They think I'm mad. That's what they say about all great writers. Anyone can write comedies. I want to write essence. Sheer sheer.

GIRL: Well, get yourself some other stooges. (*Sitting*) We're quitting you.

BOY: (*Sitting*) Comedy or nothing.

PLAYWRIGHT: I'll show you. I don't need *you* any more than those others. I'll write my play without scenery. Without lights. Without actors. Without audience. Without characters. I'll show the world. Just essence, that's all. Sheer sheer. (*Playwright stalks off toward right. Just before exiting, he turns and looks at characters*)

PLAYWRIGHT: (*Almost crying*) Damn it to Hell anyway. (*Playwright exits. After a moment, the characters talk*)

GIRL: Mad.

BOY: Simply mad.

GIRL: He'll be in a terrible mood tomorrow. But the next day he'll be O.K. again.

BOY: Yeah, then we'll all begin working like crazy on that comedy.

GIRL: We'll be terrific in it, won't we. Especially in that second act disguise scene.

BOY: I wonder if it's ever been done before?

GIRL: Who cares? The audience will love it. And that's all that matters. Essence, hah!

BOY: Sheer sheer. Hah!

GIRL: He's certainly mad, all right.

BOY: Yeah, mad as they come! (*Both begin to laugh uproariously and hit their sides as the curtains close*)

THE END

THE REWARD

THE REWARD

CHARACTERS

The Queen
The Lady
The Lord
The Traitor

Place: Private chamber of the Queen.
Time: The Past.

THE REWARD

(As the scene opens we see the Queen alone, looking into a full-length mirror at the left. She frowns at what she sees. The QUEEN is middle-aged, plain, and has an animal sensuality about her. There is a table downstage center. After a moment, the Lady enters from the right. The LADY is somewhat younger, and is also plain. She seems fearful)

LADY: Your highness, Lord Roseberry awaits without.

QUEEN: (*Turning*) Have him enter. (*The Lady turns to go*)

QUEEN: And Lady, after you've escorted Lord Roseberry in, you may leave the quarters. Give instructions that I'm not to be disturbed this evening by anyone.

LADY: Yes, your highness, I understand.

QUEEN: (*Sharply*) You understand what!

LADY: (*Fearfully*) I'll show his lordship in. (*The Lady exits right and soon reappears with the Lord. She then glances fearfully at the Queen and exits right. The LORD is elderly.*)

LORD: Your majesty.

QUEEN: Have all my orders been carried out?

LORD: To the letter. (*The Queen crosses right*)

QUEEN: (*Angrily*) Traitors! These men. Traitors to me and the kingdom. How could such a thing have happened!

LORD: Only a few know of this matter, your highness, and *their* mouths are being silenced. Some by gold and some by other means.

QUEEN: And the four culprits?

LORD: To be poisoned. Quietly at their meals tonight. Their bodies will be secreted away in the early hours of the morning. None of the citizens need ever know of this little . . . *irritation.*

QUEEN: (*Turning left*) You are to be congratulated, Lord Roseberry, on your handling of this irksome affair.

LORD: Thank you, your majesty. But, if I may speak boldly . . .

QUEEN: You may.

LORD: This desire of yours to speak with the leader is, I feel, somewhat rash.

QUEEN: You've brought him with you?

LORD: Yes, he's just outside.

QUEEN: Good.

LORD: If you'll permit me to take him back with the others, then he'll . . . *depart* with them . . . at dinner.

QUEEN: Did you bring some of the poison with you?

LORD: Yes. As you instructed.

QUEEN: Give it to me. (*The Lord hands the poison to the Queen*)

LORD: Your majesty, I am extremely uneasy.

QUEEN: But why? This poison, you know that it is *effective?*

LORD: In about an hour's time after taking.

QUEEN: And absolutely tasteless?

LORD: Absolutely.

QUEEN: And painless?

LORD: The victim drops into a sleep from which he never awakens.

QUEEN: You may leave me now, Lord Roseberry. And send in this young man.

LORD: Please, your majesty, let him die with the others.

QUEEN: He will die here with me.

LORD: I don't under . . .

QUEEN: (*Quickly*) Observe. (*The Queen pours the powder into a goblet which is on the table*)

QUEEN: When the young man enters I shall have him drink this. Then, interview him. In an hour he'll be dead.

LORD: But your majesty, the risk . . .

QUEEN: Come in the morning, Lord Roseberry, and dispose of the body. (*Turning left*) Now, good evening. (*Lord Roseberry bows, then leaves the room shaking his head. A moment later, the traitor enters. The TRAITOR is in his early twenties, handsome, and of good physique. He is somewhat arrogant in manner as he first talks with the Queen. The Queen looks at him coldly.*)

QUEEN: Come over here, closer.

TRAITOR: Your . . .

QUEEN: (*Quickly*) No, don't say it. (*Sarcastically*) Court etiquette is surely an inconsequential matter with traitors.

TRAITOR: Why have they brought me here? To *you?*

QUEEN: Because it was my desire.

TRAITOR: But why? They've learned everything about me. I suppose I'll die in some quick mysterious manner, and no one will ever know. The usual fate, I believe, of traitors.

QUEEN: (*Lightly*) Please, let's not talk of such sombre matters. What is your name?

TRAITOR: Edward.

QUEEN: (*Repeating*) Edward. Edward, please draw the drapes for me (*Edward is puzzled, but goes and draws the back drapes. As he does so, the Queen pours some wine into the glass containing the poison. She holds the goblet up to him*)

QUEEN: Now, come and take your reward.

TRAITOR: Reward?

QUEEN: Wine. To make your blood run faster. (*Edward takes the cup from her hand and looks at it*)

TRAITOR: I am close enough to kill you.

QUEEN: (*Teasingly*) But you won't.

TRAITOR: I suppose there are a dozen eyes watching us.

QUEEN: Drink the good wine.

TRAITOR: But why?

QUEEN: I've told you. As a reward.

TRAITOR: For what? Betraying you?

QUEEN: Not as a reward for the past, dear Edward, but as a reward for the present. (*Edward does not understand. The Queen steps closer to him, puts her hand up under his blouse, and runs her hand across his chest. Edward is surprised, but then begins to smile*)

TRAITOR: So this is the fate of your prisoners?

QUEEN: Some of them. The younger ones. Come, drink. It is a cold night. (*Edward drinks deeply*)

TRAITOR: The reward. It was good.

QUEEN: (*Softly*) Put down the goblet. And come into my arms. (*Edward does so. He begins to kiss the Queen, but she turns her head*)

QUEEN: Not yet.

TRAITOR: Why am *I* the one so honored. You've never seen *me* before.

QUEEN: During the questioning, I looked at all of you through a secret paneling.

TRAITOR: And you *liked* what you saw?

QUEEN: I liked you. (*The Queen begins to open Edward's blouse. Edward smiles*)

QUEEN: (*Softly*) It is a warm night. (*The Queen, with both hands, spreads back the blouse and exposes Edward's manly chest. The Queen looks at Edward for a moment, then embraces him. Edwards puts his arms around her*)

TRAITOR: (*Sensuously*) How long does *this* continue?

QUEEN: Until you become drowsy. (*Turning left*) Come, Edward, into my chamber.

TRAITOR: But your majesty, your reputation . . .

QUEEN: There is no one alive who can say that I am not . . . a Virgin Queen. Come, Edward. . . . (*The Queen exits into her chamber left. Edward stands a moment, then follows her with great expectations*)

THE END

THE VISITOR

THE VISITOR

CHARACTERS

George Crawford
Mollie Crawford
Bill Denning

Place: Living room of the Crawford home
Time: After World War II

THE VISITOR

(The scene opens on a living room set. It is well-furnished middle class. An entranceway to the outside is located upstage right. To the left upstage there is a door leading to other parts of the house. Dowstage right there are two chairs facing one another. A divan is to be found downstage left. Also downstage left there is a mirror hanging on the wall. George Crawford is looking into this mirror as the curtains part. GEORGE is in his late forties, the relic of a once robust man. There is something unusual in the appearance of George, as if he were suffering from a strange illness of some kind. After the curtains have parted, George continues to look at himself in the mirror, and runs his hands over his features in close scrutiny. After a moment has passed, George crosses the stage to downstage right and looks out the window. What he sees seems to annoy him. He then goes to a cabinet located against the wall right and takes out several large unframed pictures of himself. He glances out the window right again and carries the pictures over to the mirror where he slowly looks at each one in succession. He then examines himself in the mirror again. There is almost a hint of "wildness" in the way George has carried through the previous actions. There is now the sound of a door opening off right, and George hastily pushes the pictures under the divan downstage left. One picture, however, remains visible in part. Mollie Crawford enters from up right. MOLLIE is the same age as her husband, but seems younger. There is also a strain noticeable in Mollie and it is obvious that she is wrestling with a problem which is very important to her. She looks at her husband who stands guiltily near the divan under which the pictures are located. Mollie notices the picture for a brief moment then steps over to the window right)

MOLLIE: Dr. Letson is such a nice man.

GEORGE: (*Spitting it out*) Doctors!

MOLLIE: You and he used to be great friends.

GEORGE: He's changed. (*Mollie turns and looks at George for a moment then turns again to look out window right*)

MOLLIE: Dr. Letson is worried about you, George. Really worried. (*Turning*) And so am I, darling. Worried.

GEORGE: It's nothing serious, Mollie. Just a little illness of some kind. I'll get over it.

MOLLIE: But it's been so long now, George. (*Stepping left*) Ever since you came home from the war. Why don't you go to one of those government hospitals and see a specialist. Perhaps it's something you picked up on one of those South Pacific islands.

GEORGE: (*Quickly*) I know what's wrong with me. (*Turning left*) Nothing a hospital can do about it.

MOLLIE: What is it, George? I'm your wife. Can't you tell me?

GEORGE: It's just the strain and exhaustion from the war. Rest is all I need.

MOLLIE: (*Stepping left*) Dr. Letson thinks you should see a . . . specialist.

GEORGE: (*Turning right sharply*) Oh, so that's what you and he had to talk about down there by his car.

MOLLIE: He said you wouldn't listen to *him,* but that you might listen to me.

GEORGE: A specialist? (*Suspiciously*) What *kind* of a specialist? (*Sitting on divan*) No, don't answer. I know.

MOLLIE: It's nothing to be ashamed of, George. You went through a hellish strain. Two long years overseas. Six months in actual jungle conflict.

GEORGE: Letson told you I should see a psychiatrist, didn't he? (*Mollie doesn't answer, but turns her head away*)

GEORGE: What do *you* think, Mrs. Crawford? Do you think your husband should see a psychiatrist?

MOLLIE :I want you to see anyone who might help. I want things back the way they were before.

GEORGE: You notice that I'm different. Is that it?

MOLLIE: No, not exactly.

GEORGE: You do. I see it. How am I different Mollie? How?

MOLLIE: Nothing physical, darling, it's just . . .

GEORGE: (*Rising*) Don't lie to me!

MOLLIE: Please, George. (*George crosses down left and circles behind the divan*)

GEORGE: Oh, I've noticed the way you've been looking at me. Ever since I came back from overseas. I detected a spark of fear in your eyes that first day home and it's been growing. Slowly day by day, until now you live in constant fear of me.

MOLLIE: That's not true!

GEORGE: How have I changed! Look at me. *How* have I changed?

MOLLIE: You're not well, George. Don't excite yourself.

GEORGE: (*Softly*) It's true. I am different. (*George walks slowly over to left and looks at himself in the mirror*)

GEORGE: My forehead has changed. Seems to be shrinking. And my nose is flattening with new lines and wrinkles on each side . . .

MOLLIE: (*Stepping left*) Stop it, George.

GEORGE: (*Ignoring Mollie*) My lips are becoming flat.

MOLLIE: Stop tormenting yourself.

GEORGE: And my shoulders seem round. See, Mollie, how my coat seems to just hang on me. (*Turning*) And these hands. (*Mollie comes forward and takes him by the hand, then leads him to the divan. They both sit*)

MOLLIE: What is it, George? What is torturing you? Please tell me. It's been on your mind ever since you came back. There between us all the time like an invisible wall. I'm your wife, George. I love you. I want to help you. Is it something that happened overseas during the war?

GEORGE: (*Slowly*) I don't know. That's the Hell of it. I just don't know. (*Mollie reaches down and pulls out the pictures*)

MOLLIE: All these pictures, George. What does it mean? You have new pictures made of yourself every week. What does it *mean?*

GEORGE: It's the only way I can tell how much I'm . . . changing.

MOLLIE: Changing. Changing. Do you fear change, my

darling? Are you worried about growing older? You needn't be. Besides, we don't change by the weeks on the calendar.

GEORGE: Let's not talk about it any more. All I need is rest. Perhaps another trip.

MOLLIE: Trips don't help, George. I'm tired of travelling. What are we running away from? What's bothering you, George?

GEORGE: Nothing, dammit! (*Rises, crosses left, and circles behind sofa*) Stop your damned snooping! Oh, I'm sorry, Mollie. I could kill myself when I say things like that. Only you can't realize what Hell I'm going through inside. (*There is a ringing of a bell*)

GEORGE: I'm not at home, Mollie. I don't want to see anyone (*Mollie gets up and crosses to the door right*)

MOLLIE: It's probably just a salesman.

GEORGE: Don't let him in. I don't want to see anyone. (*Mollie exits right and George tosses the pictures under the divan again. After a moment Mollie reenters*)

MOLLIE: (*Brightly*) You'll never guess, darling. Someone from your old outfit is here. His name is Denning.

GEORGE: Denning!

MOLLIE: Said you were overseas together. In the Pacific. He'll be in as soon as he sees about his taxi.

GEORGE: I don't want to see him.

MOLLIE: What!

GEORGE: I don't want to see anyone I knew over there! Anyone from the past.

MOLLIE: But George, that's not natural.

GEORGE: I'm going upstairs, Mollie. Tell him I'm not home. That I'm away. (*George starts for the door left, but is stopped by the entrance of Bill Denning who enters the room. DENNING is in his late twenties, average looking, but seems strangely aged for his youth. He doesn't smile when he sees George*)

DENNING: Captain Crawford.

GEORGE: (*Turning*) It's Mr. Crawford now. I see that you, also, are out of the army.

DENNING: Yes, no more Sergeant Denning. At least not until the next war.

MOLLIE: I'm so glad you stopped by, Mr. Denning. I know my husband must be thrilled seeing someone from his old outfit. You're the very first one who's visited us.

DENNING: I'm on my way to California. When I got in here to Chicago I discovered I had a three hour lay-over so I thought real hard to see if I had any acquaintances I might look up between trains. Downtown Chicago is *too* much to suffer, even for three hours. So after thinking for a few moments, I remembered you, Captain Crawford.

GEORGE: Mr. Crawford, please.

DENNING: Oh, yes, I forgot. It's not easy to think of you as a civilian when I remember you so *vividly* as a company officer.

MOLLIE: Were you with my husband all during the war?

DENNING: Just part of it. When the fighting was thickest and when we needed leadership the most.

GEORGE: I'm certain, Denning, that my wife doesn't care to hear about . . . these things.

MOLLIE: Oh, but I do, George (*To Denning*) Please sit down. You know, Mr. Denning, George never mentions a word about his life in the army. One would think he'd never been in the service or gone overseas at all. (*Denning sits in chair down right. Mollie sits on divan left*)

DENNING: There are many who don't care to talk about their war experiences. Often for various reasons.

GEORGE: What time does your train leave, Denning? I'm going downtown in a few minutes—an appointment, you know, and I could drop you off. You won't have to keep your taxi waiting.

MOLLIE: George Crawford! Whatever appointment you may have can wait. But, anyway, Mr. Denning, you must let George take you back to the station when you're ready to leave. (*Rising*) I'll step out and . . .

DENNING: No, I don't want to be any trouble, and I told the cab driver if he waited I'd go back with him. So, you see how it is. (*Mollie sits again*)

GEORGE: You're leaving on the five o'clock for California?

DENNING: Yes. The five o'clock.

MOLLIE: My, that doesn't give us any time at all, does it?

DENNING: I had a little difficulty finding you. You weren't listed in the telephone directory.

MOLLIE: No, George had the telephone removed after he came back. Its ringing made him nervous.

DENNING: Oh?

MOLLIE: George has had a little sick spell, but he's coming out of it now.

DENNING: Really?

MOLLIE: My, here I am sitting when I should be mixing cocktails. (*Mollie rises*)

DENNING: Straight whiskey for me, if you don't mind.

MOLLIE: Of course not. You're not just making it easy for me, are you, Mr. Denning, because I'd be very happy to mix you something.

DENNING: I drink all my drinks straight. Ever since the war. Just whiskey and straight.

MOLLIE: And you, George. The usual cocktail?

GEORGE: No, bring me in some whiskey too.

MOLLIE: At this hour?

GEORGE: (*Coldly*) If your guest has selected whiskey, then I should be sociable and have whiskey with him. Don't you think so, darling?

DENNING: Oh, don't do anything on my account, Captain . . . I mean, Mr. Crawford. As I recall, *gin* was your favorite.

MOLLIE: Why, I'd forgotten. George, you always drank gin before the war, but since you've come back you've never had it. I believe there's a bottle in the kitchen.

GEORGE: No gin, dammit! (*It is obvious that Mollie is hurt, but she tries not to show it and turns toward the kitchen*)

MOLLIE: I'll be back in just a moment. (*Both men eye one another coldly until Mollie is out of the room through door up left, then George steps quickly toward Denning*)

GEORGE: What do you want, Denning?

DENNING: Want?

GEORGE: You know what I mean! Why did you come here?

DENNING: It's like I say, Captain. I was just passing through Chicago.

GEORGE: That's a lie. You came here to look at me. To check on me. To see if I'd changed. That's it, isn't it?

DENNING: (*Smiling*) If only the others could see you now. Cringing, actually cringing. The proud, arrogant Captain Crawford.

GEORGE: (*Softly*) Get out of my house, Denning. (*Mollie reenters before Denning can answer. She is carrying a tray. George turns and crosses left*)

MOLLIE: Here you are. Drinks for the victorious warriors. (*Denning takes a glass off the tray and drains it immediately. Mollie is a little shocked, but goes on to carry the tray over to George who takes his drink without drinking it immediately*)

GEORGE: (*Sarcastically*) You'd better go and bring the *bottle* in, Mollie.

DENNING: Don't bother, Mrs. Crawford. (*Looking around*) How quiet and peaceful it is here. Not like the jungle, is it, Mr. Crawford?

GEORGE: It's a little different.

MOLLIE: George never would tell me about those island jungles. (*Sitting on divan left*) I've always wanted to see one. In peace time, of course.

GEORGE: (*Abruptly*) Nothing to see.

DENNING: Oh, you're wrong. There's a lot to see, a lot to see, hear and smell. I never knew it could get so quiet as this in Chicago. So quiet that thinking and remembering comes easily. Remembering. I wonder if Joe Adams and Chuck Hamblin and the others are remembering.

MOLLIE: Those are friends of yours and my husband's?

DENNING: Friends of *mine*. Buddies. But they're dead. Murdered in the jungle. Their bodies still out there rotting in the black, jungle mud.

MOLLIE: Oh, I'm so sorry.

DENNING: Do you remember them, Captain? I could never forget them. Just farm kids. From Ohio. Young and clean. Strong. With smiles and a helping hand for any who needed it.

GEORGE: I say leave the dead with the dead. War's war and the less said the better.

MOLLIE: Why, George!

DENNING: (*Rising*) It gives a guy a funny feeling in the pit of his stomach when he wonders about his friends who were killed there in the jungle beside him. Wondering what they'd be doing now if they were alive. Joe Adams'd probably be back on the farm with his family, and Chuck, why Chuck would be married to that pretty little girl he was in love with. The one with auburn hair and green eyes. Chuck always carried her picture in his shirt pocket—the one over his heart. They'd have had a couple of kids by now.

GEORGE: Don't be morbid. (*George crosses to downstage left*)

DENNING: Instead he and Joe are buried out there in the jungle. The wet, stinking jungle with its disease and rot. With black, shiney-skinned snakes, huge squint-eyed birds of all kinds, and screeching hairy monkeys . . . (*George seems to freeze at the mention of monkeys. He turns toward Denning with controlled anger*)

GEORGE: If you're going to catch that train, Denning, you'd better be on your way. Traffic begins to get bad this time of day.

DENNING: Oh, I'll make it all right. Besides, there'll be other trains. There are always other trains . . . for those who are living. Isn't that so?

MOLLIE: Did you really see the monkeys, Mr. Denning?

DENNING: The jungle was lousey with them.

MOLLIE: I wish you'd sent me home one, George.

GEORGE: Damned filthy animals!

MOLLIE: I would have loved one. All my life I've wanted a monkey. Even as a girl.

DENNING: Crawford, why don't you get the Missus a monkey?

GEORGE: (*Controlled*) You son of a bitch. (*Denning smiles, then turns, and seems to be ready to leave*)

MOLLIE (*Rising*) No, don't go, Mr. Denning. Something's

very strange here. You musn't leave yet. What is it that's between you? It's something to do with monkeys, isn't it?

GEORGE: It's nothing. Let him go.

MOLLIE: Something about monkeys, and the jungle, and the war overseas.

DENNING: I'm glad to have met you, Mrs. Crawford. The taxi's waiting.

MOLLIE: No, I won't let you go until I know more . . . about this.

GEORGE: Let him leave, Mollie. Good riddance!

MOLLIE: George, you've never been like this before in your life. So upset. Now, I know what's been wrong with you all this time. It's something that happened over there. Something Mr. Denning knows about.

GEORGE: It's nothing. As for that monkey stuff, it's just a little joke some of the boys played on me, and I've never liked it at all.

MOLLIE: What kind of a joke was it, George? You, Mr. Denning, you tell me.

DENNING: (*Slowly*) It was no joke.

GEORGE: (*Controlled*) God Dammit, I say it was.

MOLLIE: Sit down, Mr. Denning. (*Denning sits again in chair right*) I want to hear about this. Something has been preying on George's mind ever since he came back. It's made a nervous wreck out of George and beginning to make one of me. (*Mollie sits on divan again*)

GEORGE: I'll tell you, Mollie, then you'll see how silly the whole thing is, and how . . . well, during the war, toward the end, things were hellish rough. The company had been out on the lines for days. The blasted Japs were everywhere. About half the company was gone. (*George cannot help meeting Denning's gaze, but quickly turns away*) One night, just about sunset, a Jap got me. I remained conscious for awhile, long enough to see all Hell was about to break loose. Then, I blacked out. Was out for a couple of days I guess, bleeding slowly all the time. When I finally came to, I was in a little hole some soldier had dug, and there were two men beside me. One was Denning.

MOLLIE: (*To Denning*) You?

GEORGE: The other fellow had been injured badly and I could see that Denning here wore a bandage on his arm. I didn't regain consciousness for several minutes, but I was conscious *enough* to feel that my arm was taped and there was a tube of some kind under the tape. I was still dazed. Thought I was in a hospital and they were giving me a transfusion. After awhile I came to and recognized Denning and this other fellow. Name was Harrison. Then I saw this . . . other thing. (*Here, George stops, seemingly overcome by his relived experience*)

MOLLIE: What other thing? What did you see, George?

GEORGE: In the hole with us was a . . . dead monkey.

MOLLIE: How horrible!

GEORGE: The monkey was sprawled up on a broken branch which had fallen into the hole. There was a rubber tube hanging down. One end was stuck into the monkey's body and the other end . . .

MOLLIE: Yes, George . . .

GEORGE: The other end had been stuck into my body.

MOLLIE: Oh, no!

GEORGE: Harrison and Denning told me that they'd used all their blood plasma before they found me and they didn't know what to do, until an injured monkey fell from the trees above. They said they had tied the screaming monkey and bled him until he died.

MOLLIE: Oh, but is it possible? I mean, is human blood like monkey blood (*Rising*) Oh, George, that was a horrible joke to play on you. Why would they do it? (*Turning right*) Why did you do it, Mr. Denning?

DENNING: It's all such a haze, Mrs. Crawford. I remember very little of it.

MOLLIE: But this other man, Harrison?

DENNING: He died several days later.

MOLLIE: Then, Mr. Denning, you're the only one who remembers this . . . this joke?

DENNING: I think it might be something your husband dreamed. True, there was a monkey in the hole with us. And there were all kinds of paraphernalia around. Tubing of some kind might have *seemed* to come from the dead monkey.

GEORGE: You lie, Denning! You rigged it up. You and Harrison with that damned hairy monkey. You hated me. You all hated me.

MOLLIE: It was a terrible thing to do to a man, Mr. Denning. When a person is injured his mind isn't right. I can't believe anyone would treat a fellow soldier like that.

DENNING: (*Starting to rise*) I'll be going now, Mrs. Crawford.

MOLLIE: No, don't. I want a drink first. George, the whiskey's in the kitchen. Bring back the bottle. (*Almost in a daze, George goes out of the room. Mollie advances left toward Denning*)

MOLLIE: Well, Mr. Denning, are you happy because of what you see? Because of you my husband is losing his mind. How far do you intend to carry this absurd joke? What made you do it? What kind of a horrible diseased mind must you have?

DENNING: What do you want me to do, Mrs. Crawford?

MOLLIE: You must tell my husband it was all a joke. You must convince him.

DENNING: He wouldn't believe me. He'd know you'd put me up to it.

MOLLIE: There's no one else who knows of this?

DENNING: Only I . . . and the dead. I hope, wherever they are, they see this and are satisfied.

MOLLIE: Satisfied!

DENNING: Sit down for a moment, Mrs. Crawford. (*Mollie sits on divan*) Your husband was the officer in charge of our outfit. He wasn't any better or any worse than the rest of them until . . . one night . . .

MOLLIE: I don't want to hear it, Mr. Denning.

DENNING: (*Rising*) There was a lull in the fighting. We knew the Japs were out there but we thought we had them pretty far away. Harrison and I and the rest of our squad were on the farthest patrol. Harrison and I, and Joe Adams, and Chuck Hamblin, Pee Wee Jones, Gord Chamberlain, Bill Noyes, and Dick Ryan. Captain Crawford, your husband, was supposed to be our leader. All our signals originated from him. He was to give the signal for advancing or retreating. Unless we heard him we couldn't move from our positions. That night about eleven o'clock the Japs pulled a sneak attack. We waited for the message, but it didn't come. The Japs began to fire and we fired back, waiting for the message—the message which never came. First, Joe was killed, then Bill, then the others, one by one. The ones who held their positions.

MOLLIE: (*Weakly*) Please don't go on.

DENNING: Harrison and I disobeyed orders and left our holes. We ran and hid, back and forth, until the Japs withdrew. Harrison held guard while I went back for help. On the way I met your husband. Half-drunk. It seems he'd become bored with the inactivity and had sneaked back to the officers' wickey for a little gin to carry him through the night. (*Mollie silently buries her face in her hand. After a moment she looks up, her face tear-stained*)

MOLLIE: And this is your revenge?

DENNING: It's almost train time.

MOLLIE: Who are you? (*Rising*) Are you a god deciding who is to be punished? Don't you think my husband would have suffered enough, just knowing about those other men? Have you no pity? Couldn't you forgive a man for weakness when he had been under such strain?

DENNING: (*Softly*) Harrison and I made a pact that we'd square things, even if it took the rest of our lives. Harrison is dead. They're all dead. (*George comes back into the room with the whiskey bottle and a glass. Mollie rushes up to him*)

MOLLIE: Guess what, darling? Mr. Denning has been telling me all about how he fixed the monkey on the branch as a joke. A joke, George. Do you hear me? Mr. Denning said it was all a joke. It was human plasma they gave you. They thought it would make you laugh when you were getting well to think about it. (*George looks slowly at Denning who makes no facial movement, then walks slowly over to the mirror and looks into it, the bottle of whiskey still in his hand*)

GEORGE: Denning lied to you, Mollie. There was only one package of plasma and he used it on Harrison. I couldn't have lived without a transfusion of some kind (*George lets the bottle slip from his hand as he examines his face in the mirror with both hands. Mollie rushes up to him*)

MOLLIE: (*Pleading*) Come away from the mirror, George. You know now it was all a joke. (*George almost savagely brushes her aside and continues to stare at himself in the mirror. Denning begins to leave. Mollie steps toward him*)

MOLLIE: Mr. Denning. (*Denning stops and looks back toward her*)

MOLLIE: (*Quietly*) You know, of course, that you'll rot in Hell for this. (*Denning looks at her, then at George, then back again at Mollie*)

DENNING: (*Thoughtfully*) Yes, I suppose I shall. (*Denning pauses a moment, then turns and exits right. Mollie stands for a moment looking after Denning, then turns slowly and gazes at George as the curtains close*)

THE END

SHOCK

SHOCK

CHARACTERS

Miss Litvak, a surgical nurse in her thirties
Dr. Goppel, a surgeon in his early forties

Place: Anteroom of a surgical room
Time: The present

SHOCK

(The scene is the anteroom of a surgical room adjoining Dr. Goppel's office. A moment after the curtains rise, Miss Litvak enters breathlessly from the surgical room, an arm over her eyes, and braces herself against the wall just left of the entranceway. MISS LITVAK is a surgical nurse in her early thirties. She is of medium stature, dark, and wears a nursing uniform complete with surgical cap. She carries a surgical mask in her hand as she enters the room, but this slips unnoticed by her to the floor as she braces herself against the wall. After a moment, she lowers her arm from her eyes and looks about. As she does so the lights come up to full for a bright moment, then fade slightly. Miss Litvak, suffering from shock, looks around the room and sees familiar objects in new, abnormal proportions. There is a table and chair down center stage. The top of the table slants and the chairs also slant weirdly. On the right there is a glass cabinet displaying surgical instruments. The cabinet seems tipsy. Upstage left is the entrance to the surgical room. The door leading to the surgical room is of a swinging variety, and is painted with mixed symbols of death and infants in death. Behind the table and chairs, upstage, is a panel on which one sees a huge, hideous eye, surrounded by dozens of other equally accusing eyes. Miss Litvak tears the surgical cap from off her head. Almost at the same time she seems to sense someone about to enter through the swinging door, so she walks—almost runs—center right. Throughout the play Miss Litvak behaves as one in deep shock. She is still a little overcome, also, with ether which escaped during the operation so that her movements are those that one coming out of an ether atmosphere might be expected to make. Dr. Goppel enters. DR. GOPPEL is an efficient looking surgeon in his early forties, tall, and well-built. He is dressed for surgery, complete with surgical cap and rubber gloves. He has caught a glimpse of Miss Litvak running from him, stops a moment, then walks slowly to the table down center. Here he takes off his mask, tosses it on the table, and turns his head slowly toward Miss Litvak. It is obvious that the doctor is also suffering from shock, but a deeper shock of guilt. Miss Litvak seems almost paralyzed with repulsion as she meets his glance).

LITVAK: (*Slowly, with controlled hatred*) You bastard. (*Dr. Goppel still looks at her with cold regard for a moment, then begins peeling off his rubber gloves. Miss Litvak takes a step forward*)

LITVAK: Yes. (*Dr. Goppel finishes removing his gloves, pauses a moment, then reaches into his pocket for a package of cigarettes. He offers one silently to Miss Litvak who continues to stare at him icily. The doctor slowly lights a cigarette and blows the smoke into air above him. Another moment passes, then the doctor slowly lets himself slip into the chair at the table, and looks blankly out in front of him. Miss Litvak approaches him*)

LITVAK: (*Softly and painfully*) Why did you do it? Why? What did you have against him? You hardly knew the boy. Just another patient. A file number with organisms. An entity of blood, bones, and cells. Why, Dr. Goppel? Why? (*Dr. Goppel draws a long breath of tobacco, then lets it escape slowly*)

LITVAK: If anyone ever finds out, you'll say it was an accident, won't you? Doctors are permitted them, aren't they? But it wasn't an accident, was it, Dr. Goppel? Your hands were steady. Abnormally steady. Your scalpel didn't slip. It was deliberate. As deliberate as all the other movements of the operation. (*Miss Litvak now stands behind the doctor*)

LITVAK: Why did you do it, Dr. Goppel? He's so young. There's so much ahead for him. (*Dr. Goppel inhales again and Miss Litvak passes to the left of him*)

LITVAK: I remember talking to him yesterday. We were waiting for you to return from lunch. He was sitting in front of a window and the sunlight streamed in and danced on his golden hair. Oh, he didn't have much to talk about. But he told me all about his girl. Her name is Anna. They're to be married next month. Did you know that, Doctor? Did you know that that boy was to be married next month? He told me he was Polish and that his girl was Polish too. Said she came from a big family and had three sisters and four brothers. We talked together then about families. He told me he was an only child and that all his life he'd been envious of people with big sprawling families, because they never knew loneliness. Then he told me he wanted a big family when he married. Did you know that, Doctor? (*Again the doctor inhales and exhales*)

LITVAK: (*Smiling*) He invited me to the wedding. He's that kind of a boy. Probably invited everyone he met to his wedding. It's to be at his girl's house, then afterwards there'll be music and dancing and more food he said than I'd ever seen before in my life. All kinds of food with all kinds of smells. He said Polish weddings were like that. Didn't make any difference whether the people were rich or poor, there was always heaping amounts of food, and red wine and lively music. Music, even if it were only somebody's grandfather squeezing away on a leaky concertina. Last night, just before I fell asleep, I decided to go to the wedding. But now, I couldn't. Everyone will be happy and gay. Did that boy invite you to the wedding? (*The doctor turns and looks at her, but doesn't speak*)

LITVAK: He liked you a lot, Dr. Goppel. Probably planned to invite you after his operation. His operation. Just a trifling thing, he said, never bothered him, but he wanted to be perfect for his girl. Just a little operation and he chose you, Dr. Goppel, to perform it for him. Perform the operation so he would go to his girl clean, and strong, and perfect. (*Miss Litvak crosses and stands behind the doctor*)

LITVAK: I should have guessed what you were thinking as I watched you standing over the operating table. You were never so strange before. Your forehead twisted and your eyes cold and grim. Savage. Yes, they were savage. You didn't look at your working fingers. Your eyes kept looking up and down over the boy who lay unconscious beneath your silver knife. It was a fine body. Strong, young, and healthy. Firm bones, bronzed muscles. You looked at it as if hypnotized. I saw hate beginning to burn in your eyes, then envy, and finally jealousy. You hated that boy because he had everything you'd never had, nor ever will have. (*Miss Litvak crosses left slowly*)

LITVAK: If I were strong I'd tell everyone I met about you. I'd tell that boy in there and the newspapers. If I had the courage I'd stand on the highest building and scream to the world your vicious crime. But I'm weak. I know it and you know it. If I breathed a word to anyone you'd have me blacklisted for life. I'd never get a job again. Perhaps if I were younger it wouldn't matter. But I'm thirty-three and a spinster. All I have is my profession. My profession! I'd always wanted to nurse, even as a little girl. I wanted to help some noble, courageous doctor in his attempts to relieve the world of a little of its agony. To make this earthly Hell of ours a little more bearable until we escape. I would have laughed then, tossed back my head and laughed, at anyone who said I might someday stand as assistant beside a crazed beast who ruined lives with little slips of a scalpel. You *are* a beast. Even more, perhaps. How does your mind work, Doctor? How did it work when you stood over that boy on the operating table? He was a nobody who would probably never amount to anything. You were a fine surgeon. Even called great by some. Yet, I know you would have given everything you possess to have been born in that boy's skin. Why, Doctor? Because he was going out into the world to become a father of children. (*Doctor Goppel flinches lightly*)

LITVAK: That cut deeply, didn't it, Dr. Goppel? But not as deeply as you cut into that boy. (*Miss Litvak steps toward right*)

LITVAK: Does it give you satisfaction to know that, in spite of his health and strength, he'll go through life sterile. Just as you? (*Dr. Goppel turns quickly toward Miss Litvak*)

LITVAK: Oh, I've known. Everyone knows. Your wife has seen to that. She wants none to think it's her fault that your marriage has been childless. (*Dr. Goppel turns in his chair and stares left*)

LITVAK: That boy in there may go through life without any children of his own. Doctor, but he won't go through life childless. He'll have sons and daughters, other peoples' kids, but he'll raise them as his own. And they'll love him, just as much as he'll love them. His body may go through the years sterile, but his spirit won't. Yours has, Doctor. Not only is your body sterile, but your soul as well. Oh, I'm not worried about our Polish boy. He'll get along all right. But I am worried about monsters like you who are free to go on living in their own tortured little worlds. (*Miss Litvak turns her back to the doctor and stares at the right wall*)

LITVAK: I should very much like to kill you. But if I did, the State would demand my death, also, and you aren't worth it. (*The eyes of Miss Litvak suddenly light on a shining scalpel in the glass case. Her eyes seem to shine for a moment*)

LITVAK: Yet . . . (*Miss Litvak goes slowly to the glass cabinet and takes out a scalpel. She grips it in her right hand and slowly approaches Dr. Goppel. Finally she reaches him and stands with the knife held above his back. For almost a moment it seems as if she is about to sink it into his back, but then she lets her hand drop and tosses the knife on the table in front of the doctor. Dr. Goppel shows no surprise at seeing the knife*)

LITVAK: No, I'll not do it. You knew I was standing behind you with that knife. You wanted me to kill you. To end your misery and torment. But, I'll not do it. Death is too good for you. I'll see that you live on. And on. I'll not leave you, Doctor, and you won't dare discharge me because of fear. Cold, trembling fear of what I might do or say. That is to be your punishment, Doctor. What a strange feeling I have. Almost as if I were God. Get up, Dr. Goppel, and see to your patient. He may be needing you. (*Dr. Goppel rises wearily to his feet. His eyes seem to be begging for mercy, but Miss Litvak remains cold and uncompromising. On his way to the swinging door, the doctor turns to look at Miss Litvak*)

LITVAK: I'll join you . . . in a moment. (*The doctor stares at her for a moment, then exits slowly through the doorway. Miss Litvak stands motionless for a moment, then sinks into the chair the doctor has just vacated, and begins to weep softly, her face buried in her arms*)

Slow Curtain

THE END

FREAK SHOW

FREAK SHOW

CHARACTERS

FATIMA
LESLIE
MR. DOPSOS

Scene: Tent Interior
Time: Evening, the present

FREAK SHOW

(The curtains part on a small carnival tent interior. Back center there is a large pole holding up center of the tent. To the right downstage is a table at which Fatima is sitting. To the left upstage is a wooden coffin supported by two tables. The lid of the coffin is raised. Upstage right is another table. Also, several chairs are around upon which are draped costumes, etc. The whole atmosphere is one of confusion and jaded carnival tatterness. FATIMA is in her early forties, blonde, pink-skinned, and weighs an enormous amount. She wears a bright, but soiled pink kimono, and is crying as the curtains open. A moment later there is a knock, followed by the entrance of Leslie from the left. LESLIE is also with the freak show, and is billed as the Half Woman/Half Man attraction. He wears masculine clothing and speaks in a deep voice)

LESLIE: Mind if I come in, Fatima? Rainy nights give me the blues—hate staying in my tent alone. (*Fatima looks up, smiles, and nods welcome*)

LESLIE: I also figgered maybe you'd be wantin' company . . .

FATIMA: It *was* getting a little lonely.

LESLIE: Ain't right you settin' here alone, Fatima. (*Looking around*) This tent's so gloomy, and that coffin there don't cheer things up any.

FATIMA: They'll be takin' it away in the morning; then Ed will be gone. Gone forever. (*Fatima puts her handkerchief to her nose*)

LESLIE: It don't seem possible Ed's dead—that he's lying there in that coffin. Why, Ed, he was so full of life. Always bustling about. It just don't seem right, him there in the coffin. And it all happening so sudden-like.

FATIMA: Ed never would take care of 'imself. Outsiders don't know them things. He'd never take pills or nothing, and he had no use for doctors. If he'd only seen the doctor earlier, he'd be here now—alive.

LESLIE: Ed was a good man, Fatima, and he loved you.

FATIMA: (*Softly*) Yes, Ed loved me.

LESLIE: How'dja meet him, Fatima? (*Leslie takes a pack of cigarettes out of a pocket and begins to smoke, after offering and being refused by Fatima*)

FATIMA: It was sort of unusual, our meeting. Fate's funny, sometimes.

LESLIE: Yeah, damned funny. (*Leslie sits in chair left*)

FATIMA: It was Christmas eve, almost twenty years ago. In a little town called Dentville. I'd just been fired from a waitress job. Too fat, they said; couldn't move fast enough for the customers. Ed was havin' coffee near the kitchen and he heard the boss firin' me. When I left, he followed and asked if I'd like a drink. At first I wouldn't speak to him because he was a stranger, but then we went to a place and had a beer. I cried into mine so much it wasn't worth drinking. When Ed left he gave me some passes to the carnival. It was in town that week. Next day, Christmas, I went over. When I saw Ed up on the platform, almost naked, I was so ashamed that I ran away before he could see me. I didn't know what he did with the carney, but I never suspicioned he'd be the tattoed man.

LESLIE: Guess it *was* a surprise.

FATIMA: When I went back to the boardin' house that evening, my suitcase was in front of the door, with a note asking me to vacate my room for someone who could pay rent. I didn't know what to do. Had no friends. Didn't know where I'd get work. Then I thought of the carnival.

LESLIE: And Ed got you in?

FATIMA: Not at first. He talked to the boss—I've forgotten what his name was. Anyway, Ed finally fixed it so I'd sell tickets at the freak show. A week later their fat lady eloped so I was offered the job. I didn't want to take it, but the regular ticket girl was coming back, so I let them put me in the show. Oh, I'll never forget that first night; all those strange people gawking at me; some of them comin' close and feelin' my skin. That's what I hated most, them feelin' my skin. (*Leslie crosses to Fatima*)

LESLIE: Your skin is so beautiful, Fatima. All soft and pink. (*Leslie runs a hand across one of Fatima's shoulders. It is a masculine gesture. Fatima seems not to notice*)

FATIMA: You should have seen it twenty years ago, Leslie. Like pink apricot skin, it was. I never used soap on it, ever. Just water, not ordinary water, but rain water that Ed would catch in a barrel 'specially for me. Ed was so proud of my skin. Flawless, he always said it was.

LESLIE: And still is, believe me.

FATIMA: Ed tried to make workin' in the show as easy as possible, but as time went by, I didn't care any more about those horrible people staring at me night after night and making those cruel jokes right in front of me, laughing like I couldn't hear 'em—like I just wasn't human.

LESLIE: We all know what that's like.

FATIMA: *You* don't have to stay with the freaks, Leslie. Why haven't you ever escaped?

LESLIE: I've tried it a couple of times, but no go. Worked as a bartender once. In a blue light joint. It was O.K. until the boss wanted me to go down for the required physical. I quit before anyone found out about me there. Another time I let my hair grow long and worked with some girls in a factory. Went fine until somebody snitched on how I had to shave every morning. (*Bitterly*) Nope, I was made for a freak show like this. Half-Man/Half-Woman. Born that way and die that way, I suppose. 'Sides, I like the people here. You, for instance. I like you very much, Fatima. I always have. Now that Ed's gone . . .

FATIMA: Poor Ed! (*Again Fatima blots her nose with a tear-stained handkerchief*)

LESLIE: Jeez, but it's creepy in here, Fatima. Shadows all around makes the place spooky as all Hell. Come over to my tent for the night. I'll get one of the boys to stay here with the coffin. Then in the morning, we can go into the main tent together and hear Ed's funeral service.

FATIMA: No, Leslie, I have to remain here. There's a reason . . .

LESLIE: It ain't right for a woman having to stay with a dead man, even if it was her husband.

FATIMA: There's a reason, a reason, Leslie. Only I can't tell you now.

LESLIE: I know it's not proper, me talking like this, with Ed still dead here in the tent, but I've a feeling he'd be all for what I'm going to say.

FATIMA: What is it, Leslie?

LESLIE: We've known one another for a long time, haven't we?

FATIMA: Yes, and we've always been good friends. Good friends, Leslie.

LESLIE: You asked me awhile back why I stayed on with the show. It's because of you I stayed, Fatima, because of you.

FATIMA: I . . .

LESLIE: No, let me talk. I'm in love with you, Fatima. If Ed were still alive, I wouldn't be saying this. But he's dead and the live ones have to go on living. That's right, ain't it, Fatima?

FATIMA: Yes, I suppose so.

LESLIE: How do you think of me, Fatima. Truthfully?

FATIMA: I don't know, Leslie. Sometimes I think of you as a sister, and then again, sometimes as a brother.

LESLIE: Could you love me?

FATIMA: As a . . .

LESLIE: As a *man,* Fatima.

FATIMA: But you're not . . .

LESLIE: Believe me, Fatima, I'm a man in . . . most ways. I have to shave, my voice is deep, and I think like a man. I could love you like a man in every way but . . .

FATIMA: Please, Leslie, don't . . .

LESLIE: Lots of couples get along without sex in their lives. We could live like that, Fatima, I know we could.

FATIMA: Ed . . .

LESLIE: Ed is dead.

FATIMA: (*Rather proudly*) Ed, oh Ed was a man in *every* way.

LESLIE: But his body, covered all over with those awful tattoos. How could you even bear to look at his body.

FATIMA: Ed always turned the lights off when he undressed so I never . . noticed.

LESLIE: But you knew, you couldn't help but know they were there—all those horrible pictures on his body—in blue and red and purple, covering every inch, leaving none of the natural white skin to show through. You, who've such lovely skin, how could you possibly stand his?

FATIMA: Ed's skin was his living. We both knew that.

LESLIE: He must have loved yours. So soft and beautiful. Like pink camellias.

FATIMA: What if my . . . skin were different?

LESLIE: In what way?

FATIMA: Oh, any way, *changed.*

LESLIE: Let's not think about that, but about *us*. After awhile Fatima, you could grow to love me as I love you. We could marry, leave the show, forget all this. I'll live as a man again. And you'll be with me, Fatima. We'll live as man and wife and we'll be happy.

FATIMA: It wouldn't work, Leslie.

LESLIE: With time it could. Maybe even by the end of the carney run this summer.

FATIMA: I may not be with the show after tomorrow.

LESLIE: What?

FATIMA: Craxton's given me notice.

LESLIE: Given you notice. Why that son of a bitch!

FATIMA: Not enough draw he said. Kept me because of Ed. Craxton wants to replace me with someone . . . weird. You see, Leslie, I'm not *weird;* I'm just fat.

LESLIE: But you can't leave. What could you do, Fatima? Where could you go?

FATIMA: I don't know. There's nothing else left but this.

LESLIE. I've met with some lousy bastards in my life, but Craxton sure takes the cake.

FATIMA: He's got the carnival to think about.

LESLIE: Well, never you mind, Fatima. Stick with the show. After awhile we'll get married. Then, in September, we'll call the carney quits and go away somewhere. Far, far away.

FATIMA: It sounds wonderful, Leslie, but it wouldn't work out.

LESLIE: Yes it would. I love you, Fatima.

FATIMA: Could you love me as Ed loved me, or as I loved him?

LESLIE: It would be easy for a man to love you, Fatima. Every man loves soft skin . . .

FATIMA: Yes, so soft and smooth. Like pink camellias. (*Leslie bends over and kisses Fatima tenderly on the neck*)

LESLIE: Say you'll marry me.

FATIMA: Have you forgotten Ed? Ed, there in his coffin. Not yet cold.

LESLIE: It's what *he'd* want, Fatima. There's nothing else for you to do.

FATIMA: There *may* be something else, Leslie. Craxton has an idea how I might be a bigger attraction.

LESLIE: How? By putting on more weight?

FATIMA: No, but never mind now.

LESLIE: Give me an answer about *us,* Fatima. Please give me an answer. I could soon mean a lot to you, maybe more than Ed. And my skin is clear and smooth, like yours, Fatima.

FATIMA: After the funeral tomorrow, Leslie, come in here and ask me again. *If* you ask me then, I'll answer yes. (*Again Leslie kisses Fatima on the neck*)

LESLIE: Of course I'll ask you, darling. What could stop me? And if Craxton keeps you in the show on account of this new gimmick, whatever it is, that'll be great.

FATIMA: I wonder if I could ever love you, Leslie. In the way I loved Ed. You're so . . . unstable.

LESLIE: I'll change, Fatima, you'll see.

FATIMA: What time is it?

LESLIE: (*Glancing at watch*) Ten o'clock, Why?

FATIMA: The man—the man Craxton's sending over—is coming at ten, so you'd better leave.

LESLIE: What man? Fatima, what man?

FATIMA: His name is Dopsos. A Mr. Dopsos.

LESLIE: Never heard of 'im. What's he coming here for?

FATIMA: You'll know tomorrow.

LESLIE: You're sure acting mysterious all of a sudden. Must be mighty important.

FATIMA: The most important thing in my life, I guess, except for the time I met Ed. Poor Ed. Now, Leslie, please go.

LESLIE: Until tomorrow, sweetheart, after the funeral. Oh, we'll be happy together. (*Again Leslie kisses Fatima on the neck and leaves left. Fatima stands and begins running her fingers caressingly over her body, sobbing slightly at the same time. A moment later Mr. Dopsos enters, carrying a small black kit. MR. DOPSOS is in his middle sixties, dark, shrivelled, and looks like an undertaker. As Mr. Dopsos passes the coffin he shudders*)

DOPSOS: Mr. Craxton said I was just to walk in—that you'd be waitin'.

FATIMA: You're Mr. Dopsos?

DOPSOS: (*Nodding*) Horrible name, ain't it?

FATIMA: (*Simply*) Life is horrible.

DOPSOS: Yep, at times it is.

FATIMA: Had you met my husband?

DOPSOS: I don't believe I had the pleasure, although I knew of his reputation.

FATIMA: He's in the coffin there. (*Mr. Dopsos turns, and nods to Fatima*)

FATIMA: Don't you want to look at him? (*Mr. Dopsos turns and fearfully approaches the coffin. What he sees startles him*)

DOPSOS: (*Turning*) Why, he's . . . *unclothed!*

FATIMA: Yes.

DOPSOS: Isn't that a bit . . . *irregular?*

FATIMA: Under some circumstances perhaps. Is it warm enough in here for you, Mr. Dopsos?

DOPSOS: Oh yes, quite. Thank you.

FATIMA: Then, if you'll help me move this chair over by the coffin, we can begin.

DOPSOS: I don't understand. (*Fatima lifts up the end of the chair upstage right. Dopsos crosses and helps her carry it near the coffin*)

FATIMA: Is there enough light, Mr. Dopsos?

DOPSOS: Yes, I believe so. Say, I don't like this job at all!

FATIMA: It's your profession, isn't it?

DOPSOS: Yes, but . . .

FATIMA: It should be easier on a woman's skin. A woman's skin is so soft.

DOPSOS: Yes, much easier. Your skin is so beautiful.

FATIMA: Like camellias? Pink camellias?

DOPSOS: Why yes, and if I might say so it's really a shame. Surely, there must be some other way . . .

FATIMA: One must live, Mr. Dopsos.

DOPSOS: But isn't there someone. Someone who might . . .

FATIMA: Might . . . love me? As a brother? As a sister? Perhaps. But as a man, a husband? (*Fatima smiles and shakes her head*)

DOPSOS: It's getting late. (*Nervously*) Now just what did you have in mind? (*Fatima points to the coffin*)

DOPSOS: You mean . . .

FATIMA: An exact copy. (*Mr. Dopsos is shocked*)

FATIMA: You can sit between me and the coffin. (*Mr. Dopsos is speechless. Fatima sits in the chair*)

FATIMA: (*Simply*) Mr. Dopsos, I loved my husband very, very much. (*After a moment, Dopsos shrugs, turns, and begins opening his little black bag. Fatima remains motionless as the curtains close*)

THE END